making artisan gelato

QUARRY

making artisan gelato

45 Recipes and Techniques for Crafting Flavor-Infused Gelato and Sorbet at Home

BEVERLY MASSACHUSETTS

QUARRY BOOKS

TORRANCE KOPFER

Photography by Madeline Polss

First published in the United States of America by
Quarry Books, a member of
Quayside Publishing Group
100 Cummings Center
Suite 406-L
Beverly, Massachusetts 01915-6101
Telephone: (978) 282-9590
Fax: (978) 283-2742
www.quarrybooks.com

Library of Congress Cataloging-in-Publication Data

Kopfer, Torrance.
  Making artisan gelato : 45 recipes and techniques for crafting flavor-infused gelato and sorbet at home /
Torrance Kopfer.
     p. cm.
  Includes index.
  ISBN-13: 978-1-59253-418-0
  ISBN-10: 1-59253-418-X
  1. Ice cream, ices, etc. 2. Frozen desserts. I. Title.
  TX795.K67 2008
  641.8'62--dc22

                                                    2008030312
                                                    CIP

ISBN-13: 978-1-59253-418-0
ISBN-10: 1-59253-418-X

10 9

Design: Silke Braun
Photography: Madeline Polss
Special thanks to Tina Wright for her editorial consultation.

Making Artisan Gelato contains a variety of tips and recommendations for making gelato. While
caution was taken to give safe recommendations, it is impossible to predict the outcome of each
recommendation or recipe. Neither Torrance Kopfer, or Cold Fusion Gelato, Inc., nor the publisher,
Quayside Publishing Group, accepts liability for any mental, financial, or physical harm that arises
from following the advice or techniques, using the procedures, or consuming the products in this
book. Readers should use personal judgment when applying the recommendations of this text.

Cold Fusion Gelato
389 Thames Street
Newport, RI 02840 USA
www.coldfusiongelato.com

Printed in China

DEDICATION

To all of my family and especially to Nola

contents

introduction

How often do we hear professional athletes, celebrities, or chefs recount how they came into their profession? Quite often it seems their tales inevitably include "All my life I wanted to do" … just what they are doing. This is not the case in my story. I didn't set out to own a gelato business. Growing up, I trained as a classical musician, and playing the violin was my "thing." Later, I enrolled at a music conservatory in New York, where after two years studying violin performance and conducting, I realized I'd rather be a patron of the arts than a starving artist. I opted for an economics degree and pursued a career on Wall Street.

One day, I realized that I was spending way more time on food websites, thinking about food, and talking to people about food, than I was on my actual job. So, I bit the bullet and made a career change—into the food world.

I bought an existing gelato business in Newport, Rhode Island, primarily for the location and its equipment. I immediately threw out all of their recipes (there was a reason it was for sale), and started to practice making gelato. I studied the craft in Italy and elsewhere in the United States, and I read everything I could about gelato, sorbet, and ice cream. I also tasted a lot of gelato, sorbet, and ice cream and learned to differentiate between the good- and the not-so-good-quality gelato. I reopened the gelato store under a new name, convinced some important folks to buy my gelato wholesale, and suddenly I was in the gelato-making business full-time.

Now my violin mostly gathers dust while I balance writing, surfing, learning to fly, being a good husband, and making the best gelato possible.

If you like ice cream but have never made it from scratch, I hope this book inspires you to try it. In selecting these recipes, I wanted to incorporate enough that seemed familiar and would not feel intimidating while still offering plenty of choices for more novel, less traditional fare. The Ingredients and Equipment chapters list all the basic requirements of gelato making, while the Techniques chapter offers step-by-step instructions for the main procedures for any gelato or sorbet recipe.

The chapter on pairing flavors and creating winning combinations touches on my suggestions for how to combine flavors in the hopes of giving you confidence to use your own imagination and creativity in the kitchen. Remember, gelato is really all about having fun while creating a tasty, frozen treat!

The word *artisan* has, to some degree, been hijacked by marketers attempting to sell inferior-quality goods at premium-quality prices. The values of an artisan must inform the creative process from inception through completion, whether we are shaping clay or making gelato. *Artisanal* means not taking shortcuts for convenience's sake, and not purchasing inferior ingredients to save a few pennies—it is deciding at every stage to place quality before all. If quality is always paramount, quality will always show in the results.

–Torrance Kopfer

PART I:

the basics

Before beginning any new endeavor, it is helpful to understand the elementary information about that particular subject. This section of the book contains exactly those fundamentals that may be useful when making gelato.

Chapter 1 begins with a brief history of gelato and includes some insight into how this frozen confection has evolved through the centuries. Chapter 2 introduces the core ingredients in a basic gelato base and the foods and products that are used in the recipes in this book. Once the initial ingredients are sourced, the next step is to set aside the correct equipment to properly peel, cut, weigh, measure, or cook those ingredients as needed, which will be explored in Chapter 3. Finally, Chapter 4 merges ingredients and equipment and includes in-depth instructions for turning simple ingredients into finished gelato.

Chapter 5 explores the types of gelato flavors that go well together, introduces theories on flavor and flavor combinations, and advises on where to find unusual flavor combinations.

Whether you are an experienced cook or relative beginner, reading through this entire section is a good idea. It will familiarize you with all the essentials before you immerse yourself in part 2, The Recipes.

CHAPTER ONE

the history of gelato

The word *gelato* is derived from the Italian verb *gelare*, meaning "to freeze." It is no surprise that the Italians are most often credited with the invention of modern-day gelato, which traces its origins to the court of the Medicis, and to Catherine de Medici in particular.

Legend has it that a chicken farmer by the name of Guiseppe Ruggieri first submitted *sorbetto* to the Medici court in a cooking contest. He concocted it from old and almost forgotten recipes and a hearty dose of his own creativity. Catherine was so enamored of the sweet, icy treat that in 1533 she took Ruggieri to France, where she soon married Henry, Duke of Orleans, and introduced the frozen treat to the French nobility. (This is where *sorbetto* came to be known as *sorbet*.)

Slightly later in the same century, a Florentine architect named Bernardo Buonatali improved on the creation by developing a method for freezing a mixture of zabaglione and fruit and served his specialty to Italian and foreign guests visiting the Medici court.

It is yet another Italian, however, who is credited with commercializing ice cream in the late seventeenth century. Using a machine invented by his grandfather, Procopio dei Coltelli combined ice and salt to freeze the dessert. He soon moved to Paris, where in 1686 he opened a shop from which to sell his much-improved version of ice cream. He was granted a special license by the king, which gave him exclusive rights to sell these icy confections. Café Procope became a popular meeting spot for the literati, and his frozen desserts were the talk of the town.

A GELATO BY ANY OTHER NAME …

While modern-day *sorbet* or *sorbetto* refers to a water-and-fruit-based mixture, historical references seem to use *gelato* and *sorbet* interchangeably. In fact, the term *gelato* is often used in Italy to reference any frozen dessert, whether milk or water based. In the most common modern definitions, *gelato* refers to milk-based mixtures and *sorbet* to nondairy gelatos, most commonly flavored with fruit.

Although most food historians can agree on this part of gelato's history, it is gelato's earlier years that remain cloudy. Some historians look to the Old Testament, claiming the cold mixture of goat's milk and ice given to Abraham by Isaac is an early reference to ice cream. Other historians look further back in time to an ancient Chinese recipe for cooked rice mixed with milk and other ingredients and buried in the snow to freeze. And what of indications that the Egyptian pharaohs offered guests chalices filled with snow and fruit juices, or that the Roman emperor Nero Claudius Caesar sent slaves to the mountains to retrieve snow and ice to cool and freeze his fruit drinks, or that Marco Polo returned from the Far East with a recipe for making water ices that resemble modern-day sherbets? And where, exactly, did Ruggieri find those old and nearly forgotten recipes for sorbet?

Needless to say, gelato and sorbet have enjoyed many influences, which were brought to Italy from around the world by explorers, traders, crusaders, and other travelers. With each incarnation, the recipes and methods were tweaked and perfected, steered by the tastes of the times, ultimately into what is enjoyed today. Gelato and sorbet as they are now known were never invented, but rather, in the strongest of Darwinian traditions, they evolved.

WHAT IS GELATO?

At its core, gelato is a mixture of milk and cream, sugar, eggs, and a flavor ingredient that is chilled and whipped while it is frozen. Gelato is created essentially the same way as ice cream and uses essentially the same ingredients, the major difference between the two being the amount of air and butterfat contained in each. Gelato contains between 6 and 8 percent butterfat, whereas American-style ice cream ranges from 10 to 16 percent. Because gelato contains less fat, less air is whipped into it when it is simultaneously churned and frozen in an ice-cream maker. Thus, gelato has a slightly denser and softer consistency than ice cream.

> ### ZABAGLIONE
>
> Zabaglione, also called *sabayon*, is a light custard cooked over a water bath while being rapidly whisked or whipped to incorporate air. A basic zabaglione recipe includes egg yolks, sugar, and a sweet liquor or wine such as Marsala. Zabaglione is traditionally served warm, with fresh fruit.

When visiting a gelateria, one notices that gelato is served from a different type of freezer and stored in a different sort of container than American-style ice cream is. Gelato freezers are of the forced-air variety. Air circulates around the gelato, holding the product at a consistent temperature and preventing it from becoming too hard. The containers holding the gelato inside the forced-air freezers are generally long and shallow rectangular bins, not the deep, large tubs that hold vast quantities of ice cream. An important part of the gelato experience is eating it as soon as possible after it has been made, so most gelaterias make relatively small batches, and consequently, the gelato is held for a much shorter period of time before it is eaten.

GELATO AT HOME

Just as with American-style ice cream, gelato in a professional setting is a much different product than gelato made at home. This is primarily due to the ice-cream freezer, the machine used to turn the liquid base into a frozen and whipped concoction.

In a commercial laboratory (as gelato kitchens are called in Italy), ice-cream freezers (professionally referred to as batch freezers) can make anywhere from 0.5 to 10 gallons (1.9 to 38 L) of gelato in about six to eight minutes. Even the most advanced home-style ice-cream freezer cannot come close to that timing. Professional ice-cream freezers also remove heat from

gelato and sorbet mix much more efficiently than home-style ice-cream makers do, thereby contributing to the minimal freezing time. The speed at which a professional machine freezes the gelato mix is the primary reason why gelato made at home is so different from what's available at your favorite gelateria.

The timing of the freezing process is crucial for one main reason: ice crystal formation and size. When making gelato and ice cream, fast freezing results in very small ice crystals. The smaller the ice crystals, and the more water that's frozen when the gelato emerges from the machine, the "drier" the end product. Commercial machines that freeze the gelato mix very quickly are generally more efficient at producing a drier gelato than can be made at home.

Ingredients also play a role in differentiating professionally made versus home-made gelato. Professional ice cream and gelato companies have access to certain ingredients consumers do not, such as certain sugars, natural stabilizers, and commercial-grade emulsifiers. These ingredients can help control the rate at which ice crystals are frozen, which then affects their overall size. Additionally, certain ingredients will also help control the quality of the finished gelato over time; for example, fruit pectin, lecithin, and vegetable gums help control water crystallization, allowing the gelato to keep its integrity if made well in advance of being eaten.

Homemade gelato offers one significant opportunity not often available in a professional setting: the ability to consume it as soon as it has finished freezing. This is when gelato is at its absolute best because at that precise moment, the gelato is as fresh as it's ever going to be. And this exact moment has nothing to do with the ingredients you have access to or the type of freezer you have or how long it takes to make the gelato in your kitchen—all this perfect moment depends on is simply you being present when the freezing just finishes, and then, with a spoon at the ready, taking that first mouthful of gelato. That is what homemade gelato is all about.

Having said that, there are a few things you can do to help maximize the quality of gelato made at home. One important success factor is to always make sure the mix is as cold as possible before putting it into the ice-cream maker. You can even stick it in the freezer for fifteen to twenty minutes before you churn it, to ensure that it is very well chilled. And if the style of machine you are using offers the option of removing the dasher, stick the dasher in the freezer as well. The colder everything is that comes into contact with the gelato mix as it is churning, the better, as it will cause ice crystals to form faster and smaller, rendering a smoother end product.

DRY FREEZE

Dryness, in a gelato or sorbet, refers to the degree to which the water within the mix is frozen. A gelato (or sorbet) is considered dry when as much of the water contained in the mix as possible is frozen when it comes out of the machine. Ideally, a finished gelato should be very smooth, solid, and quite dry. Wet gelato is gelato that after being processed in an ice-cream freezer for a set amount of time still has not been frozen solid. It looks soft and slightly melted.

CHAPTER TWO

ingredients

What *is* gelato, and from what is it made? While the answer might seem quite obvious, it is important to have an understanding of the gelato base or mix as well as the different roles that each ingredient plays in the final, exquisite confection.

From a scientific standpoint, gelato is a frozen, sweetened emulsion. Generally, gelato is created by combining liquids (such as milk and cream) that are sweetened with sugars (such as cane sugar or honey) and flavored with any number of palate-pleasing substances (such as strawberries or vanilla bean). Combining ingredients in the proper order, with the proper techniques, and in the proper proportions will help the gelato base (or mix) hold air while being frozen.

> **TIP** › The terms *base* and *mix* are used interchangeably to refer to gelato while it's in the liquid form, before it is put into the ice-cream freezer.

The major ingredients of gelato base all play specific roles, and understanding these roles is essential to creating an overall successful recipe. When considering a mix, two questions must first be answered: what are the components necessary for a flavorful mix and how do the individual ingredients supply these essential components?

This chapter addresses these questions by first breaking down the five primary components, then exploring general ingredients and how they supply some or all of these components when making high-quality gelato. Consequently, the component section has a bit more geek-speak in it than the rest of the chapter does—the science of each component is explained. True, understanding gelato on a scientific level is not crucial to successfully making gelato. However, if you have a clear understanding of the role each ingredient plays, you succeed in creating and experimenting with flavors not in this book.

THE FIVE BASIC COMPONENTS

All basic mixes, either for gelato or ice cream, contain five major components: water, sugar, fat, solids, and flavoring agents. For gelato (or ice cream or sorbet) to behave properly when it's frozen (i.e., not too stiff or too runny, thick enough to hold air, and so on), the mix must contain balanced percentages of all its components. A balanced gelato mix will have the following percentages: fats, 6 to 11 percent; sugar, 16 to 21 percent; solids, 30 to 38 percent; and water and flavoring agents, the remaining percentage. (See chart on page 20.)

Fats	6%–11%
Sugar	16%–21%
Solids	30%–38%
Water/Flavor	30%–48%

It is not necessary to create exact percentages of all the components in your gelato, but understanding ingredients in context will improve gelato making. More important than achieving exact percentages is maintaining their balanced ranges. I include them here to illustrate ingredients in terms of the role they play in the aforementioned categories.

Water Content

Nearly every gelato ingredient has some degree of water content. It is not often added to recipes in a home setting (other than to sorbets), but it is essential to keep overall water content in mind as a gelato mix takes form. In making gelato's frozen emulsion, the combination of fat and water allows air to be whipped into the mix, and this same combination of fat and water suspends air bubbles as the mix freezes.

If an ingredient contains an excessive amount of water, the imbalance of fats and water may make a smooth texture harder to achieve, and whipping air into the gelato will be difficult.

One way to control the percentage of water in the base is by adding more fat. Fat offsets the effect of increased water content. Another solution is to cook down the liquid ingredients (fruit or alcohol, for example), creating a reduction.

Similar to a reduction, creating concentrated versions of liquid ingredients manages a base's overall percentage of water. Citrus zest can be steeped in and heated with the milk, providing a potent citrus flavor without additional juice, thus keeping the mix balanced.

WATER BALANCING ACT

Water is an important factor to keep in mind when experimenting with flavors on one's own. For instance, to make an orange gelato, one might think to use orange juice. However, because orange juice is essentially water, large ice crystals will form during the orange gelato–making process, causing the final product to freeze solid and be hard to scoop.

Conversely, water is a completely different animal, so to speak, in making sorbet. By definition, sorbet is fruit, water, and sugar. Without water to thin the fruit purée, the components would be imbalanced, and the mix would freeze too solid to be scoopable.

Clockwise from top: turbinado sugar, raw sugar, light brown sugar, dark brown sugar, white sugar

Sugar

Sugar enhances flavor, improves the texture and the palatability of the gelato, and is often the cheapest source of solids available. (This is aside, of course, from its role in sweetening the mix, putting the "dessert" in frozen dessert.) Sugar's other role is in lowering, or depressing, the freezing point of the mix. Water freezes at 32°F (0°C). Gelato, because of the addition of sugar, freezes at a temperature lower than 32°F (0°C), allowing it to be scoopable at colder temperatures without turning the gelato into a solid block of ice.

Another important role that sugar plays is in the way it can heighten the potency of certain ingredients. Adding sugar to mediocre raspberries and allowing them to macerate will make those raspberries taste ripe in a matter of minutes.

Sugar can come from many different sources. Milk has natural sugars in it (lactose, specifically), and fruits also have sugars that can come into play. For the most part, none of these sugars is terribly important in a home setting (as opposed to a commercial setting), but it's good to remember when experimenting.

Most sweeteners (which, for the purposes of this book, refers primarily to sugar) range from 16 percent sweetness on the very, very low side to 21 percent or so by weight. Sweetness in this instance refers to the percentage of sugar by weight in the overall mix. In a professional artisan setting, and definitely in a home setting, the majority of this sugar comes from regular table sugar. If sugar composes 16 to 21 percent of the total recipe weight, the other 79 to 84 percent is water, other solids (from fruit, etc.), and milk solids and fat. Bear in mind, however, that this is not a hard-and-fast rule—there is room for variation with these percentages in a home setting.

Fat

Let's just get this out of the way right now—this is a book about rich-tasting, lusciously creamy gelato. The great thing about gelato, however, is that while it still tastes deliciously decadent, it has less fat than ice cream does. Taste real gelato next to a fat-free version, though, and you will instantly understand why fat is important! Whether making ice cream or gelato, there needs to be some fat in the product—it can't be helped. A good rule to remember is, "Everything in moderation," and that applies to fat in gelato as well. (A flavorful lower-fat alternative is sorbet, which is naturally fat-free.)

The role fat plays is why gelato (and ice cream) has a rich, thick, creamy texture. Additionally, fat helps transmit flavors that are oil soluble, and it enhances the overall flavor profile of the gelato. Fat's other job is to help create and maintain the emulsion that ensures the mix will be frozen properly. Water molecules are suspended within the fat molecules, stabilizing the mix and allowing the emulsion to trap air as it is whipped. The trapped air creates volume as the liquid mix is frozen into gelato. When creating a gelato or ice cream recipe, one important aspect is creating a mix that will hold air as it is whipped, while it is simultaneously being frozen. The presence of fat in the mix is what helps significantly with this process.

And lastly, fat can also help keep the gelato from becoming grainy by curbing excessive ice-crystal growth.

Gelato's fat can be contributed by myriad sources: nuts and nut oils, other flavoring agents, and primarily from dairy ingredients and eggs.

Solids

Solids are not necessarily an intuitive component of frozen dessert, but they do serve a vital role. The definition of solids is somewhat self-explanatory; they refer to anything that isn't a fat or water. Sugar

---

EXPERIMENTING ON SOLID GROUND

Understanding the role of fats and solids is helpful when experimenting with different flavors and ingredients, as these can have a big effect on the outcome. For instance, if you decide to modify a recipe slightly, trying a different main flavor ingredient than originally called for, the finished gelato may freeze as hard as a rock. The cause of this undesirable outcome may be simply having too many solids in the mix. Knowing the role of solids will allow you to adjust and experiment with your recipe accordingly.

---

is considered a source of pure solids (i.e., just about 100 percent solids), and fruits, nuts, spices, and even milk all contribute solids in one form or another.

The solids in the gelato mix improve the texture of the finished gelato; they give it body and add the slightly chewy consistency that gelato and ice cream can have. That texture, known as "mouthfeel" in a professional setting, determines how the gelato feels in your mouth—smooth, creamy, icy, grainy, and so on. And, like fats, solids also help gelato hold air while it is whipped and frozen.

TIP › The air that is whipped into and held by the mix during the freezing process is referred to as *overrun* in geek-speak.

Unusual tastes you would not ordinarily think of for desserts can be used to give gelato a pleasing flavor.

Flavoring Agents

A flavoring agent is, quite simply, anything that can be used to add flavor to gelato. Flavoring agents come from just about anywhere—fruits, extracts, spices, or teas, to name a few. Anything with flavor of its own can be used.

Finding appropriate methods for adding flavoring agents is a matter of understanding what the flavor is, where or how it is found, and then determining how best to extract that flavor from its original medium and incorporate it into the gelato base. This can be done by puréeing the ingredient, steeping it in milk or cream, or using a natural extract, for example.

Where creativity comes into play is in deciding how to get the flavor from its original source into the gelato. How does one get Earl Grey tea's distinctive bergamot flavor, for example, into a gelato? Grinding tea leaves and stirring them directly into the mix might create an unappetizing texture. Instead, tea bags can be steeped in the milk used to make the base.

Remember that the flavoring agent will not only add the desired flavor, but will most likely provide some sort of solids content as well (not to mention more water, depending on the end flavor and the ingredients used to get there).

ESSENTIAL GELATO INGREDIENTS

Once the components (or building blocks) of a gelato base are understood, the ways the individual ingredients contribute to these components can be explored. While it might seem appropriate to sort ingredients into their respective "families"—fruit, dairy, eggs, and so on—thinking about the ingredients in fixed categories creates complications.

Each ingredient contains multiple components and thus plays multiple roles. Milk, for example, brings multiple characteristics to the party. It contains water, butterfat, sugar, and solids: each is a component found in a complete mix. Milk's role in gelato is therefore complex. Relating individual ingredients to their components and roles helps decipher the balance and chemistry of the gelato mix itself.

> **TIP ›** When buying ingredients—for any recipe, not just gelato—live by this golden rule: the quality should be paramount. The quality of ingredients has a direct correlation to the quality of flavor.

The Components of Basic Gelato Ingredients

The following chart lists typical gelato ingredients and indicates what primary components, or traits, each adds to the gelato mixture.

	Water	Sugar	Fat	Solid	Flavoring Agent
Alcohol	X	Possibly			X
Chocolate		X	X	X	
Cocoa nibs					X (as inclusion)
Cocoa powder			X	X	X
Corn syrup	X	X		X	
Cream	X	X	X	X	
Eggs	X		X	X	
Fruit	X	X			X
Milk	X	X	X	X	
Nuts			X	X	
Salt				X	
Sour cream	X		X		
Spices					X
Sugar		X		X	

Alcohol

Alcohol can add a touch of elegance or sauciness to frozen desserts. It can also be a superior carrier of flavor; alcohol distills and extracts many flavor elements better than water does.

Adding alcohol, however, will result in a softer end product because alcohol depresses the mix's freezing point. The same lower freezing point that allows you to chill vodka in the freezer will prevent a gelato from reaching the same hardness at a given temperature. Unless the alcohol is cooked off completely during preparation, the gelato will be softened by its lower freezing point. This can be a helpful trait for a gelato

TIP › When selecting alcohol to add to recipes, try to choose something that would be appealing on its own as a drink and that is of relatively good quality. Do not ruin a delightful homemade frozen concoction with rotgut whiskey. That said, don't take out a second mortgage on the house for a bottle of 1947 Château Petrus for a blackberry cabernet sorbet! (In case you are considering a bottle of Château Petrus, be forewarned: anything as fine as a 1947 Petrus will only be sullied by the addition of blackberries!)

that tends to freeze harder, such as a flavor with chocolate base. Too much alcohol, however, and the gelato (or sorbet) just won't freeze.

Chocolate

With so many brands and qualities of chocolate available, infinite gelato variations can be made. There are three main types of chocolate: white, milk, and dark. Within those types, choosing a brand hinges on personal taste and matching the properties of what is called for in a specific recipe.

WHITE CHOCOLATE

For a long time, white chocolate was not actually considered chocolate because it is made from ingredients other than "real" chocolate: pure cocoa butter and sugar. Some white chocolate has vanilla or vanilla flavor added, creating its trademark flavor. White chocolate is now officially considered chocolate (at least by U.S. FDA standards) when its cocoa butter content is not less than 20 percent of its total weight.

MILK CHOCOLATE

Milk chocolate is differentiated by the addition of milk to the chocolate and does not have as strong a cocoa taste as dark chocolate does. In any of the recipes in this book, milk chocolate can be substituted for dark chocolate if a less intense, sweeter finished product is preferred. Milk chocolate, depending on the manufacturer, has anywhere from 32 to 45 percent chocolate (or cocoa bean) content, outweighing other ingredients such as sugar, lecithin, and vanilla.

DARK CHOCOLATE

Dark chocolate is also referred to as semisweet or bittersweet chocolate by most cooks. These chocolates are darker in color and have a more intense chocolate flavor. Semisweet and bittersweet varieties can be used interchangeably, with bittersweet imparting the stronger chocolate flavor. Bittersweet chocolate typically ranges between 52 and 99 percent chocolate/cocoa bean content.

UNSWEETENED CHOCOLATE

Unsweetened chocolate is 100 percent pure, dark chocolate with no other ingredients added. This type of chocolate imparts an intense dark chocolate taste to any recipe.

COATING CHOCOLATE

This type of chocolate is often less expensive and includes other ingredients, such as vegetable oils or fats, not found in pure chocolate. Chocolate chips may be considered coating chocolate. These chocolate products are formulated for a certain, more mainstream role in the food universe, and consequently, they may add other flavors to gelato that may or may not be desired.

Top to bottom: milk chocolate, dark chocolate, white chocolate, coating chocolate

Cocoa nibs

Varying shades of cocoa powders

Cocoa Nibs

Cocoa nibs are intense chocolatey bits of the cocoa bean. They are small and crunchy and can be mixed into gelato for a bitter, chocolatey crunch.

Cocoa Powder

Always use good-quality cocoa powder. Dutch-processed powder creates a deeper, more rounded chocolate taste, but all the recipes in this book that call for cocoa powder will not be compromised with regular cocoa powder. Dutch-processed cocoa is cocoa powder that has been treated to counteract its natural acidity, neutralizing it slightly. (Non-Dutch-processed cocoa might have an unpleasant acidic/astringent note.) If a cocoa powder is Dutch-processed (it is not listed on the package), baking soda (sodium bicarbonate) will be in the ingredient list.

Corn Syrup

Corn syrup is an invert sugar, which is a sucrose molecule that has been altered so that the fructose and glucose molecules are split apart. This usually happens with the introduction of an acid during the heating process. Invert sugars tend to have a slightly higher sweetening power than regular table or granulated sugar. Therefore, if one gelato were made with regular sugar and another were made with an equal amount of invert sugar, the one with invert sugar will be slightly sweeter. Invert sugar also has a greater antifreezing property. In short, the same amount of invert sugar versus regular sugar will keep the product softer and sweeter at any given temperature than if it were made with regular sugar.

Whenever a recipe calls for corn syrup, use light not dark, unless otherwise specified.

Cream

Cream is usually the primary way to add the needed amount of fat to the gelato. There are many different types of cream available, differentiated by their butterfat content. Half-and-half can contain anywhere from 10.5 to 18 percent butterfat, light cream from 18 to 30 percent butterfat, whipping cream or light whipping cream from 30 to 36 percent, and heavy cream from 36 percent and up. Pasteurized cream has been heated to 181°F (83°C) for one minute and then cooled. Ultrapasteurized cream has been heated to 230°F (110°C) for one second and then cooled.

> **TIP ›** A little secret that ice-cream manufacturers might not want you to know: some commercial ice creams have pure butter added to them. This decision is driven by the bottom line, not necessarily flavor: tinkering with butter allows commercial manufacturers to hit their target fat content more cost effectively than if cream were used.

Corn syrups and honey

Whole milk and heavy cream

Eggs

Egg yolks were originally used in ice cream and gelato for their stabilizing and emulsifying properties. In commercial settings today, other ingredients such as carrageenan and guar gum are more widely available and effective. More prevalent in a home setting, where professional-grade stabilizers are not as accessible (or necessary), eggs are still used for a couple of different reasons.

Of primary importance is their protein content. When an egg is heated, its proteins are denatured, creating longer strings of protein molecules and therefore longer strands of protein. This, in turn, thickens the egg, as well as anything else that the egg has been added to. This thickness helps the gelato hold air as it is being whipped and frozen. Without some thickness to the base, the ice-cream maker is going to have a hard time getting the base to "hold on" to any of the air that is being whipped into it while it is being frozen.

Eggs also contain lecithin, a natural emulsifier that helps bind liquids into a stable mix. This also helps retard the natural tendency of an emulsion to separate, making it more stable. So in a way, lecithin is a natural stabilizing agent. And finally, egg yolks are an important source of solids within the gelato base.

When it comes to egg safety, commercially purchased eggs are generally extremely safe. However, to alleviate any concerns about cooking the eggs enough, or to be on the completely safe side, you can purchase eggs that have been pasteurized in their shells.

TIP › Dairy ingredients are a perfect food source for bacteria because milk products tend to be highly nutrient-rich environments. To avoid unwanted bacteria in the mix, make sure the eggs and milk products reach a minimum temperature of 165°F (74°C) when cooking the custard for the base. This temperature should kill the vast majority of any bacteria present. (This is where an instant-read thermometer comes in quite handy.)

Milk

The primary ingredient of most gelato is milk, not the heavy cream that is usually found in American-style ice cream. Milk comprises a water component, some natural sugars, natural fats, and some solids. Recipes in this book that call for milk use whole milk only. It is possible (although not recommended) to use skim milk or milk with a lower fat percentage, however, the gelato will be grainier and less smooth because milk other than whole milk does not contain a high enough amount of fat. If lactose intolerance is a concern, lactose-free milk is an option, as long as it has the same amount of fat per serving as whole milk does. Also, there are enzyme drops that can be added to the milk to make it more digestible for those who have trouble with lactose. Bear in mind, though, that because lactose is a sugar, an additional 1 to 2 tablespoons (13 to 26 g) of sugar may need to be added to the recipe to keep the antifreezing properties in balance.

To avoid using dairy altogether, substituting nondairy milks, such as rice and soy milk, is also an option. However, the recipe will need to be adjusted to compensate for the lack of fat. In this instance, adding one to three egg yolks and possibly some cornstarch (approximately two teaspoons [9 g]) will help thicken the mix. The cornstarch should be whisked into the egg yolks when making the custard.

COMPENSATING FOR LOWER-FAT DAIRY

The main challenges with replacing milk or heavy cream in a recipe is thickening the mix and replicating the creamy mouthfeel. Since a large part of the mouthfeel comes from the fat contained in the ingredients in the recipe, one would have to figure out how to replace that function: which ingredient(s) or component(s) can be incorporated instead of milk or cream? Soy milk has a small amount of fat and has a slightly greater viscosity than regular whole milk, so it is a viable option. Natural nut oils may also supplement the fat content (if the nut flavor complements the gelato flavor).

Fruit

Its imperative when using fresh fruit that it be very, very ripe. It should not be rotten, mind you; just be sure it's plump, that it yields to the touch, and, depending on the type of fruit, that it's very fragrant. It should be evident that the fruit is nice and juicy. Fruit is perfect for gelato and sorbet when it is bordering on overripe.

While fresh is always best, if choosing between underripe fresh fruit and frozen fruit, choose frozen.

TIP › If you don't have access to perfectly ripe fruit (or if the desired fruit is out of season), a good alternative is frozen fruit. As strange as this may sound, fruit that has been frozen ahead of time tends to be the ripest fruit available in the grocery store. This is because, in most cases, the fruit was picked at its peak of ripeness, rendering it too ripe to transport without being frozen.

Nuts

Nuts used for gelato (or any quality foodstuff) must be fresh, not spoiled or rancid. Unfortunately, rancid nuts look the same on the outside as fresh ones. So, test them by tasting them—it's the only way to really tell. Pop one into your mouth and bite into it. If it makes you want to immediately spit it across the kitchen, chances are it's rancid and others should be tested. If there are a few rancid nuts in one batch, there is a very high likelihood that most, if not all of the other nuts, will also be rancid (or headed there very quickly).

All nuts are subject to spoiling, some more easily than others. Pecans, macadamias, walnuts, and hazelnuts are among the more susceptible types, as they have a higher oil content than some of their less oily (and thus, less susceptible), cousins, such as almonds and peanuts.

If purchasing nuts in bulk, try to find a source that sells tons of them and has a high turnover to ensure they are not old or likely to turn rancid shortly after purchasing. Storing nuts in the refrigerator or freezer extends their shelf life.

Salt

While many of the recipes in this book call for salt, this does not mean the gelato will taste salty. Salt sharpens certain flavors, and a pinch is usually all that is required. Kosher salt is preferred to table salt. Kosher salt has a larger, looser crystalline structure and lower salinity than table salt, which is more forgiving when cooking, so oversalting is less of a worry. Although table salt will suffice, because it is "saltier" than Kosher salt, be sure to use a bit less than the recipe calls for.

ADDING RAW SALT

Raw salt can be added to gelato or sorbet right before it is served, creating an interesting sweet/salty combination. Try to find a salt with larger, flaky salt crystals, and make sure to use a light touch. There should just be a hint of sweet/salty interplay.

Clockwise from top: smoked salt, black sea salt, Kosher salt, flake sea salt

Left to right: curry powder, cardamom pods, cinnamon sticks, ground chipotle

Sour Cream

When selecting sour cream for a recipe, try to find one that contains as few ingredients as possible. Crème fraîche can also be used. Bear in mind, however, that crème fraîche will give the finished gelato a richer, rounder, and less tangy taste than sour cream. Low-fat versions of sour cream can be substituted, but they will add a small amount of water to the mix (although not so much that it's of tremendous concern).

Spices

As with nuts, freshness is the key. As spices age, they lose their flavor and pungency. It's important to source the highest quality possible, and don't buy large amounts if you are not going to use them in a timely fashion. Buy smaller quantities and replace them frequently. Try to keep spices in a cool and dark spot as well. It's tempting to store them next to the stove, but this is one of the worst spots for spices, as cupboards around stoves tend to be quite warm. Storing spices in the freezer will slow the aging process, depending on how volatile the oils contained in the spice are.

Sugar

For the most of the recipes in this book, granulated sugar is the preferred sweetener. Most of the sugar sold to home bakers is cane sugar, derived from sugar cane. Beet sugar, which is refined from sugar beets, may be available regionally, where sugar beets are grown. From the gelato-maker's perspective, beet sugar functions exactly like cane sugar. Organic sugar is perfectly acceptable to use as well, and the use of organic sugar should result in virtually no change in taste or freezing performance. Any variation in taste from organic sugar is a result of the degree to which the organic sugar has been refined.

> **A SUGAR OF A DIFFERENT COLOR**
> When making gelato, light brown, dark brown, or raw sugar can all be used. The basic difference between these is the addition of molasses, which is usually removed during the sugar-refining process. Raw sugar and light brown sugar still contain molasses, so the finished gelato will display some of that flavor profile. Dark brown sugar has molasses added back into it, which will create an even stronger flavor profile in the finished product. Because using any of these types of sugar will add the taste of molasses to the end product, it's a personal choice whether to use them or not.

> **TIP ›** Whole spices and herbs can be steeped in milk or cream before being used in gelato. Bring 1 to 2 cups (240 to 475 ml) heavy cream, light cream, or half-and-half to a boil. Remove from heat and add 3 to 6 tablespoons (18 to 26 g) of the spice, or approximately 3 to 6 ounces (85 to 170 g) of the fresh herb to the heated cream. Stir, cover, and let steep for ½ hour. Strain out the herb or spice, and the infused cream can be added to a gelato base to add a particular flavor.

Mix-ins

Mix-ins apply to anything and everything that is mixed into the gelato before it has finished freezing in the ice-cream maker. A trick from the professionals: freeze all mix-ins before they are added to the mix. When room-temperature mix-ins are added, they melt the gelato immediately surrounding them. These margins then refreeze, creating large ice crystals, and therefore adversely affecting the overall texture of the finished gelato.

CHAPTER THREE

equipment

Making gelato or sorbet at home should not require a huge investment in equipment. In fact, most of the smaller items, such as strainers, knives, and measuring cups, are likely already in your equipment arsenal. If investing in new equipment, however, research all options first. While a general rule is to buy the best quality of each item you can, depending on your overall budget, a savvy shopper will soon understand where to "cheat". For example, measuring cups, can vary in price by several dollars per set. The cups' sturdiness, accuracy, and the readability of the measurements are more important than their cost. A good-quality knife, however, is worth its weight in gold.

This chapter explores most of the equipment needed to make gelato. The largest expenditure a first-time gelato maker will likely have is an ice-cream maker. Luckily, there are numerous choices available today, depending on your needs, preferences, and budget.

ICE-CREAM MAKERS

When considering home ice-cream makers, there are three nonprofessional-grade styles.

Old-Fashioned Style

One style widely available and simple to use is the old-fashioned type with the big plastic or wooden outer bucket and a metal interior bucket. The instruction manual for any machine always goes into more elaborate detail on how it works, but a quick overview follows: the ice-cream mix is first placed in the inner bucket. The dasher (the part that whips air into the mix as it is being frozen) is then inserted, and that entire contraption is set inside the outer bucket. Enough ice and rock salt are subsequently added to the outer bucket to completely surround the inner bucket. Typically these buckets have a 1-gallon (3.8 L) capacity.

Depending on the make of the particular ice-cream machine, the motor's electrical cord is plugged in to an electrical outlet or the hand crank is attached. Either initiates the churning process. As the motor turns (or you turn) the dasher inside the cylinder is manually turned, air is whipped into the product, and eventually you get ice cream.

The benefits of the old-fashioned style of machine are that not only are they relatively inexpensive, but the quantity of ice cream that can be made in a home setting is substantial, as long as there is enough ice and rock salt on hand.

The cons, however, are in the manual hand cranking of the dasher and the time it takes the mix to freeze. Several people must be willing to help with the churning to ensure a successful batch. However, the electric versions are noisy, and the motor is at risk of burning out if it is not tended to properly. The motor can no longer turn the dasher once the ice cream freezes hard. If the machine is not turned off immediately, the motor will burn out.

Left: Italian-made gelato machine, right: Standard ice-cream maker

Prefrozen Cylinders

The style of home ice-cream maker most widely available on the market has a cylinder that needs to be prefrozen before the mix is added. The cylinder is double walled and filled with a liquid that, once it has been frozen solid, stays cold for a long period of time. Generally, the machine is assembled with the dasher attached. The frozen cylinder is inserted, the machine turned on, and the gelato or sorbet mix poured in while the machine is running. If the mix is poured into the frozen cylinder while the motor isn't running, the mix will freeze so quickly that the motor won't be strong enough to turn the dasher, sabotaging the process.

This style of ice-cream maker is popular as it is relatively affordable and easy to operate. However, bear in mind that with this style, there needs to be enough room in the freezer for chilling the cylinder. Only one batch of gelato can be made every twenty-four hours because the cylinder thaws each time it is used and needs to be fully frozen again before it is reused. You absolutely cannot cheat this step unless you have a freezer that runs at temperatures deeply below freezing. The cylinder needs to be completely frozen solid for the gelato or sorbet mix to freeze in the ice-cream maker. Therefore, it can be difficult to make multiple flavors or larger quantities for a party, unless multiple cylinders are purchased.

Self-Contained Freezers

Another style of ice-cream maker has a self-contained refrigeration system. This is the most convenient option, as multiple batches of gelato can be made as long as a power source is available to generate an endless supply of refrigeration—no cylinder pre-freezing is required. Unfortunately, along with being the most expensive option, this style can also be heavy and cumbersome to move, and these machines take up a fair amount of counter space. These are also not easy to clean, as the entire unit can't simply be thrown into the sink.

Professional Ice-Cream Makers

In comparison to what's available for the home setting, commercial freezers have extremely powerful motors with enormous compressors relative to the size of the machine itself. These motors are what drive the dasher, which turns inside the cylinder containing the gelato mix, thereby allowing air to be whipped into the mix as it freezes. The speed at which this process occurs allows the mix to freeze quickly and efficiently. Big commercial freezers are also usually water cooled, making them more efficient since water transfers heat faster and more effectively than air.

PACOJET: THE CRÈME DE LA (ICE CREAM) CRÈME

If you have ever had ice cream at a fancy restaurant, it may very well have been made with a high-end, professional-grade machine available almost exclusively to chefs, such as a Pacojet. A base or mix is first made, and then, unlike when using a traditional ice-cream freezer, frozen solid in a canister custom fitted to the machine. The canister, filled with its frozen mix, is next inserted into the machine.

An arm, similar to a spindle but with many tiny blades at its end, spins at a very high speed and shaves down the frozen mix so it is the consistency of ice cream.

Chefs like this particular machine as it can be used for both savory and sweet options and offers the opportunity to make one serving at a time versus an entire batch, allowing for optimal freshness.

Assorted strainers and heavy-bottomed saucepans

SAUCEPANS

Spend a few extra dollars for a good-quality, heavy-bottomed saucepan. The heavier the pan, the more even the heat distribution. Not only will this alleviate scorching or scalding when heating milk and cream or making the custard for the gelato base, but a well-made saucepan will endure a lifetime of use.

STRAINERS

Strainers can be found in myriad shapes and sizes, and having at least two on hand—one with medium mesh and the other with fine mesh—is recommended. It is always better to use a strainer that is slightly larger than one that is too small or with too tight a mesh, which renders it difficult to pass a mixture through. Generally, it is easier to push a mixture through a strainer with rounded mesh than conical mesh. And a good, heavy-duty handle is imperative so that the strainer doesn't bend when the basket is full.

BLENDERS

Blenders come in two styles, countertop and stick, or immersion, blenders. A countertop blender has a tall, lidded glass or plastic container that sits on a base containing the motor and the controls for the machine. Items or mixtures are placed into the container, and when the machine is turned on, the blades at the bottom of the container spin and chop, mix, or purée from the bottom up, and all contents are thoroughly mixed. Also known as stand blenders, these styles have powerful motors and are best for puréeing denser items such as fruit.

A stick, or immersion, blender is a handheld, versatile appliance that is placed inside the mixture being blended (in its own container). Relatively new to the consumer marketplace, these have been gaining in popularity for their ease of use. The benefits of this type of blender is that it is small, lightweight, and easily portable; it can be used to homogenize custard cooking on the stovetop, for example. The main drawback is that the motor of an immersion blender is not very powerful, so the volume and type of product that can be easily blended is limited.

FOOD PROCESSOR

Similar to a stand blender, a food processor can have an even stronger motor and may sometimes be the better option for chopping or puréeing items. Food processors differ from stand blenders in that they have multiple blade options; a shorter, wider container, which allows product more access to the blade when being chopped or puréed; and an opening at the top through which to continuously add ingredients or product without interrupting the processing. Additionally, one can easily change the blade in a food processor midway through blending. Most food processors have a larger capacity than stand blenders, so they are better for larger-volume recipes.

Left: food processor; right: stand or countertop blender; front: stick or immersion blender

FOOD MILL

A food mill is an alternative way to purée fruits and vegetables. To use a food mill, the desired food is placed into the mill and the hand crank turned until the batch has been pushed through a screen. The screens are interchangeable, and they are available in a range of mesh sizes. By changing the screens each time the item is pushed through, starting with the largest mesh and working down to the finest, the item becomes smoother and smoother, until the desired consistency is reached.

OTHER SMALL EQUIPMENT

A kitchen that is well equipped for gelato making will also have some of the following small pieces of equipment. Many, such as measuring spoons, spatulas, and whisks, are considered kitchen staples, whereas others, such as scales, zesters, and juicers, can be considered helpful but not necessarily essential.

China Basket

Also called a spider, this tool is perfect for scooping fruit from boiling water or an ice bath. Its wide, slightly rounded basket holds more than a large spoon, and its wire or mesh stainless steel surface drains all unwanted liquid. If your local kitchen store does not carry this implement, try sourcing it through a Chinese restaurant supplier.

Food mill

Left to right: balloon whisk, piano or French whisk, China basket, assorted spatulas, wooden spoon

Spatula

Spatulas are invaluable for mixing, cooking, and scraping mixtures from mixing bowls and other containers. Invest in a good, heatproof spatula (such as one made from silicone). Several sizes should be kept on hand, though the wider ones are often more versatile than the smaller, narrow kind.

Whisks

There are two basic types of whisks on the market: the piano or French-style whisk and the balloon whisk. The piano or French style is longer and narrower. A balloon whisk is more rounded, like its namesake. Because of this shape, balloon whisks are used when more air or volume is needed in a mixture. For the recipes in this book, using a piano or French-style whisk is recommended, as it is not necessary to incorporate much air into the gelato and sorbet bases.

The choice of whisk handle (metal, plastic, or other material) is a personal one.

Wooden Spoon

Just like whisks and spatulas, wooden spoons should be a staple in the equipment arsenal. They are great for stirring sauces, mixing batters, and, most important, cooking custards. Wooden spoons can be found in assorted shapes and sizes, from almost flat to deep and rounded. If purchasing only one or two, choose a style that is neither flat nor overly rounded, and one that feels comfortable in the hand.

Knives

A high-quality sharp knife is important to have. It is not crucial for the actual making of gelato, but it will come in handy when preparing fruit and other ingredients. As a general rule, the price of a professional knife is directly related to the quality of that knife. Therefore, it pays to spend a little more to get a superior knife. A good knife will have a heavy, solid grip or handle and an equally heavy-feeling blade. It's important to hold a knife and practice maneuvering it before buying it. Don't be scared or intimidated by a long, sharp blade. If the knife is comfortable and fits the hand, careless cuts are unlikely.

The two most versatile knives (at least for these recipes) are an 8 or 10-inch (20 or 25 cm) chef's knife and a paring knife. The chef's knife is perfect for larger tasks, such as coring pineapple and chopping chocolate, whereas the paring knife can be used for almost every other fruit and ingredient preparation, from scraping the seeds from a vanilla bean to peeling the skin off a peach. Also, always keep knives clean and sharp!

Chef's knife and a small slicer

Glass mixing bowls in assorted sizes

Mixing Bowls

Mixing bowls are made in an array of materials, including glass, stainless steel, and plastic, among others. Stainless-steel or glass bowls conduct both heat and cold well; a hot custard poured into a stainless-steel mixing bowl over an ice bath will cool down much more rapidly than if poured into a plastic container placed over the same ice bath. Glass bowls allow the mixture to be monitored during mixing, too.

Zesters, Graters, and Peelers

To some extent, these all accomplish the same general task: they remove the peel or skin from fruits and vegetables. What differentiates the three is the degree of fineness achieved by zesting, grating, or peeling skin.

A zester will render the finest, smallest particles of fruit or vegetable skin, or whatever one chooses to zest. In recent years, Microplane zesters have taken over as the tool of choice. This is a style of zester

> **TIP** › Here's a trick to keep your mixing bowl from moving around when whisking a mixture: Dampen a hand towel, and if necessary, wring out any excess water. Then twist it around in a coil and wind it around the base of the mixing bowl, fitting it snugly against the bottom of the bowl. The dampness of the towel will prevent it from sliding around on the counter and the mixing bowl will be anchored. (Placing a silicone pot holder under a mixing bowl will accomplish the same goal.)

that shaves off a tiny amount of the item being zested. Microplane zesters are very sharp, however, so beware of zesting your fingers by mistake. Look for one that has a good, sturdy handle and feels solid enough to withstand the pressure applied against it when zesting.

Another type of zester is used when long, very thin strands of peel are desired. This type of zester resembles a fork with small, sharp cylinders at the end of the tines. These tines are pressed into the peel and dragged across the fruit while applying firm and even pressure, cutting through the top layer.

The box grater is a common style of grater, and these generally have four grating planes that dictate the size and volume of the grated ingredient. They stand upright on a counter (or cutting board) and therefore can withstand a range of pressure or jostling during grating.

A peeler is a handheld implement used when large pieces of fruit or vegetable skin need to be removed. They are available in long, narrow styles as well as shorter, wider ones. The blades tend to dull quickly, which then causes the peeler to slip, so be sure to always have a sharp peeler handy.

Juicer

Fresh fruit juice is always preferable to concentrate or frozen purée, as long as the fruit is in season and at its ripest. An elaborate, expensive juicer is not needed for the small quantities called for in the recipes in this book. A hand juicer works just fine and is affordable and easy to use and clean. It may take a bit more elbow grease, but the results are well worth it. Just remember to strain fresh juice to remove any unwanted particles, such as seeds.

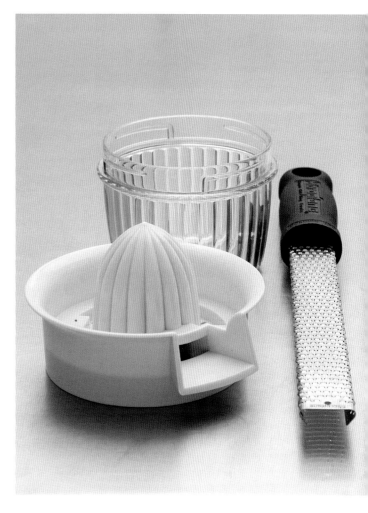

Left: hand juicer; right: Microplane zester

Back: glass liquid measuring cups; front left: metal dry ingredient measuring cups; front right: metal measuring spoons

Measuring Cups and Spoons

There are two types of measuring cups: those that measure dry ingredients and those that measure wet. Each style better facilitates accurate measurement of its ingredient. Dry measuring cups are made of metal or plastic and look like little saucepans with long handles. These are used to measure dry ingredients such as flour and sugar, and allow for a more accurate and consistent measure in two ways. First, the dry ingredients can be scooped by the measuring cup itself, eliminating the need to pack it in by hand, possibly adding more weight than the desired amount. Second, the top of the rim is used to level the ingredient, minimizing over- or underscooping.

Wet-ingredient measures are suitable for all types of liquid and resemble large, wide mugs with a handle on one side. Most are made of clear glass or plastic and have imperial and metric units printed on the outside of the container. Because these measuring cups are transparent, it is easy to accurately measure wet ingredients by filling the cup to the desired line of measurement.

Sets of measuring spoons can be found in metal or plastic and usually range from ⅛ teaspoon to 1 tablespoon (0.6 to 15 ml) measurements. These are used to measure small quantities of both wet and dry ingredients.

Kitchen Scale

Professional chefs prefer using scales to measuring cups and spoons for the simple reason that scales are the most accurate means to measure ingredients consistently. Two people can measure one scoop of flour into a dry measuring cup and, chances are, those two scoops of flour will have different weights, based solely on how each person scooped the flour. However, the same two people can each weigh 1 pound (455 g) of flour on a scale and they will each

have 1 pound (455 g) of flour. Because this same inaccuracy applies to volume as well, professional recipes almost always provide all measurements in weight.

If investing in a scale, a digital scale that allows measuring in both imperial and metric units offers the most versatility (and therefore the most use).

Thermometer

For the same reasons they use a scale for accuracy, chefs often use a thermometer to ensure that ingredients are cooked to the desired temperature.

A digital, instant-read thermometer is convenient and easy to read, and many affordable, simple models are available. Traditional (mercury-based) cooking thermometers function by being inserted into the cooking liquid and waiting a short while for the temperature to register. An instant-read thermometer measures temperature in seconds, so it will never get in the way of cooking or other procedures, such as steadily mixing custard while it cooks.

Candy thermometers are useful when cooking sugar or making caramel. Most home-style candy thermometers consist of a glass thermometer inside a metal frame. To use one of these properly, insert it into the center of the mix and wait several minutes before reading to get the most accurate temperature. Always store a candy thermometer upright; never lay it flat in a drawer, as this may cause it to decalibrate.

Storage Containers

Always keep a freezer-safe dish or container handy for hardening off the freshly made gelato. This simply means placing a plastic or glass dish, bowl, or storage container with a tight-fitting lid in the freezer ahead of time to chill. Because this dish will be quite cold when the finished gelato or sorbet is added, little to no surface melting will occur upon contact.

CHAPTER FOUR

techniques

Mastering these procedures or skills allows chefs and home cooks to experiment and create their own concoctions. Once you know and understand the basic methods used to create what you are preparing, you are less bound to a written recipe. Recipes call for multiple cooking techniques that dictate how ingredients will combine into a desired outcome. Poor execution of an important technique can result in a less desirable finished product, so I encourage you to read this section carefully and follow the directions as precisely as possible. With time and practice, the techniques listed in this section will become second nature and can easily be incorporated into other areas of your cooking repertoire beyond gelato and sorbet.

ENHANCING UNDERRIPE FRUIT

The flavor of fruit that is not as ripe as it could be can be enhanced by a simple technique called maceration. Add a small portion of the sugar specified in the recipe to the fruit, mix gently, and let macerate overnight before the fruit is puréed. This will improve the overall flavor of the fruit and therefore the finished product.

Macerating the fruit in sugar creates fruit syrup that can then be added to the gelato or sorbet, imparting a fuller fruit flavor. When fruit is at its ripest, the natural sugars are most developed. In today's world of intercontinental shipping and 24/7 availability, unless fruit is purchased straight from the orchard in season, its quality isn't necessarily the best. Most fruit is picked while still green enough to withstand the rigors of transport and storage before landing on the supermarket shelf. Because the natural sugars never had the chance to develop fully, macerating the fruit helps mimic the natural ripening process.

Under-ripe, perfectly ripe, and over-ripe bananas

THE SCIENCE OF RIPENING

Underripe fruit can be allowed to ripen after it has been picked. The degree to which fruit will ripen, however, is directly proportional to how much natural starch is in the fruit. This is why bananas, which are starchy, ripen a lot after picking and citrus not at all. To boost the ripening process, place fruit in a paper bag, add an apple, and fold down the top of the bag to close. Apples release a gas (ethylene) that helps ripen fruit. This works well with bananas and avocados.

MACERATING FRUIT WITH SUGAR

Add a small portion of sugar to the fruit.

Mix the fruit gently, and let macerate overnight.

Berries

Common types of berries include raspberries, blackberries, blueberries, cranberries, strawberries, and huckleberries. Before puréeing, berries should be rinsed thoroughly to remove any dirt or pesticides and drained of excess water. To rinse berries, simply place them in a strainer and run under cold water, shaking the strainer slightly to allow the water to wash over all the berries.

Seed Fruit

While all fruits contain seeds, seed fruits, for the purpose of these recipes, are fruits that have seeds embedded in the center of their flesh, including melons, papayas, and grapes. When preparing a fruit such as a melon or papaya, in which the seeds are large and accessible, slice the entire fruit in half, remove the center seeds with a large spoon and discard them. Slice the half into sections. The fruit meat should be sliced from the outer rind and cubed, the rind discarded, and only the fruit meat reserved for making the purée.

When making grape purée, use a seedless variety to save time and painstaking preparation. If seeded grapes are the only option, slice each grape in half and remove the seeds with the tip of a knife. Grapes can be peeled or not, depending on the texture desired in the finished gelato or sorbet. Leaving the grapes unpeeled allows the grape skins to add texture to the finished product. (Peeling grapes also takes a tremendous amount of time and effort.)

> **TIP** › Although it might be tempting to obliterate the grapes, seeds and all, in a blender and then strain the liquid, doing so causes the seeds to be ground up, releasing a very bitter and unpleasant taste.

PREPARING FRUIT FOR PURÉEING

Different types of fruit require different preparation methods before they can be puréed into a liquid. Some fruits have pits or stones that need to be removed, whereas others have tough skins or outer shells. If it is not clear how to prepare a fruit, a good rule of thumb is: remove whatever part of the fruit would not normally be eaten. If it doesn't taste good raw, it's not going to taste good in gelato or sorbet.

PREPARING SEED FRUIT

Slice the entire fruit in half.

Remove the center seeds with a large spoon.

Slice the fruit meat from the outer rind.

Slice or cube the fruit meat.

Stone Fruit

Stone fruit is any fruit that has an inedible center pit or stone. This includes apricots, peaches, plums, nectarines, and cherries.

Fruits with smaller center stones, such as cherries, do not need to be peeled. Cherries can be pitted with a cherry pitter or sliced in half and pitted with the tip of a knife.

To remove the center stone from fruit such as apricots, peaches, plums, and nectarines, gently guide the blade of a sharp paring knife into the fruit until it hits the center stone. Holding the fruit in one hand and the knife in the other, carefully rotate the fruit around the blade of the knife, holding the knife steady while cutting through the flesh of the fruit. Rotate the fruit completely to return to the starting cut and remove the knife. Grasp the fruit with both hands and gently turn each hand in the opposite direction, twisting the fruit apart into two halves, with the stone or pit remaining in one half. Depending on how ripe the fruit, it may be necessary to gently rock the halves back and forth before you twist them apart to loosen the fruit meat from the stone. Remove the pit with a spoon or knife and discard.

PREPARING STONE FRUIT

Insert the blade of a sharp paring knife into the fruit until it hits the center stone.

Carefully rotate the fruit around the blade of the knife.

Gently turn each hand in the opposite direction, twisting the fruit apart into two halves.

Remove the pit with a spoon or knife and discard.

SLICING A MANGO

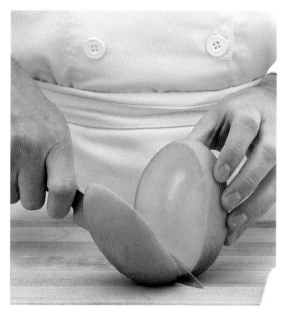

Slice off the plump sides of the mango as close to the center stone as possible.

Score the mango meat into cubes, slicing all the way through the meat but not through the mango peel.

Pop the meat from the peel by bending back the peel and pushing out the meat.

Scoop out the meat.

With larger stone fruits such as mangoes, it's easier to remove the fruit from the stone than vice versa. Start by slicing off the plump sides of the mango as close to the center stone as possible. Next, score the mango meat into cubes, slicing all the way through the meat but not through the mango peel. Then simply "pop" the meat from the peel by bending back the peel and pushing out the meat. Scoop out the meat, discard the peel, and repeat with the other side of the mango.

NOVELTY KITCHEN TOOLS

These days it is easy to find specialized, novelty tools in high-end kitchen stores and boutiques. Tools now exist to peel bananas, remove stones from mangoes and slice and core an apple, to name just a few. And while none of these are truly necessary, they may make your job easier and save some preparation time.

An alternate method of working with a mango is to first peel it. Use a sharp paring knife for this. Start at the top of the mango and make a small cut into the peel, just until you hit the fruit meat. Insert the knife blade under the peel and, holding on to the outside of the peel with your thumb, pull the peel away from the stone and down at the same time. Repeat until the mango is fully peeled. Then simply slice the meat off the stone and dice as necessary.

Citrus Fruit

Citrus fruit are oranges, lemons, limes, grapefruit, and tangerines. Most citrus fruit does not need to be puréed. Instead, zest the skin, reserving it for mixing in later, then cut the fruit in half and juice it.

The zest can be added to the sugar when making sorbet or gelato, stirred into the mix just before being poured into the ice-cream machine, or added as a garnish to the finished product. Zest infuses any recipe with a potent citrus flavor from the natural oils stored in the skin. Often, the natural oils in citrus zest enhance and intensify the flavor of a frozen citrus dessert, in a manner that the juice alone could not.

JUICING A LEMON

Press down on the fruit and roll under palm of hand to release juice.

Cut the fruit in half and juice each half.

Begin by cutting off the bottom.

Follow by cutting off the top.

Slice lengthwise from the top of the pineapple to the bottom.

Quarter the pineapple lengthwise.

Cut the harder core out of the center.

Slice the fruit into smaller pieces before processing.

Puréeing Other Favorite Fruit

This encompasses any other type of fruit that is used in gelato and sorbet and is not categorized elsewhere.

APPLES

Apples, of course, should always be cored, and the core discarded. To peel or not to peel an apple is a personal choice. Depending on the type used, the skin could add color and texture to your finished gelato or sorbet.

PINEAPPLE

Pineapples need to be both peeled and cored. The easiest way to peel a pineapple is to cut off the top and bottom, so that the pineapple stands flat and even when upright. Next, starting at the top, insert the blade of a knife just under the pineapple skin, between the outer skin and the pineapple meat, and gently slice lengthwise from the top of the pineapple to the bottom. Be sure to slice deep enough to remove the eyes but not so deep that too much fruit is cut away. Follow the natural curve of the fruit, removing just the skin of the fruit. Once fully peeled, split the pineapple in half from top to bottom and then quarter lengthwise. Cut the harder core out of the center of each quarter and discard, leaving the softer, edible part of the fruit. Slice the fruit into smaller pieces before processing.

PEELING STONE FRUIT

Score the fruit with a sharp paring knife.

Boil fruit for about 1 minute.

Plunge boiled fruit into the ice bath to cool the fruit instantly.

Use a sharp knife to peel off the skin easily.

PEELING STONE FRUIT

Before removing the stone from the fruit flesh, decide whether the skin of the fruit should be peeled. Although including the fruit peel in the recipe can add texture and flavor, be mindful of whether that particular flavor and texture would enhance or detract from the finished gelato or sorbet. Many fruit skins and peels have a bitter element to their taste. Additionally, serving gelato or sorbet at a formal dinner party versus a summer picnic might dictate how refined a consistency is expected.

For stone fruit such as apricots, peaches, nectarines, and plums, an easy way to peel them is as follows: Prepare an ice bath in a bowl large enough to accommodate two to three whole fruit at a time. Bring a large pot of water to a rolling boil. Score the fruit with a sharp paring knife. Gently drop two to three pieces of fruit at a time into the water and boil them for about 1 minute. (Peaches and nectarines are particularly sensitive to being overcooked; if in hot water for too long, the flesh will become mushy.) Remove the fruit from the hot water with a slotted spoon and immediately plunge into the ice bath. This will cool the fruit instantly, and the skin will peel off easily.

> **TIP** › When using hot water to loosen the peel from fruit, it is imperative that the water remain at a constant boil. If the stove top power is too weak or the pot being used is small, err on the side of only dropping in one or two pieces of fruit at a time.

PURÉEING FRUIT

Fruit is added to a blender (or food processor) for puréeing.

The texture of the purée can be monitored between pulses, ensuring a desirable consistency.

STRAINING FRUIT

Fruit purée can be poured into a sieve or strainer to remove particles of fruit or blended matter not desirable for the final preparation.

The liquid purée is strained, and what remains in the sieve can be discarded.

PURÉEING FRUIT IN A FOOD MILL

Small fruit, such as blackberries, can be puréed whole in a food mill.

If using a food mill, the fruit is pushed through a mill by manually turning the crank.

MAKING FRUIT PURÉE

Puréeing fruit is a simple process once all the advance preparation has been done. Before placing into a blender or food processor, large fruit should be cut into small chunks so it has easier access to the blades. Small fruit, such as blueberries, can be puréed whole.

Process the fruit in the blender until all or most of the chunks are gone, depending on the desired texture in the finished gelato. The type of blender being used will determine what speed or function is used to purée. If using a food mill, larger fruit must first be diced. Push the fruit through the mill by manually turning the crank. Repeat this step several times as needed, changing the screens from coarser to finer to break down all the fruit and remove as much of the liquid as possible.

After the fruit has been blended, it may be necessary to strain it. Straining the puréed fruit removes any leftover pieces of skin, membrane, unprocessed fruit, or any particles that may have been puréed by mistake. The idea is to press only the liquid through, leaving behind any remaining seeds or stems. Straining is recommended, as it creates an overall consistent texture in the finished gelato. To strain, pour the purée into a fine- or medium-mesh sieve or strainer placed over a mixing bowl.

Use the back of a ladle or a spatula to firmly press the purée against the inside of the strainer, pushing as much of the liquid through as possible. Discard whatever is left in the strainer after all the liquid has been released.

Storing Fruit Purée

Fruit purée should be stored in a clean, airtight container in the refrigerator until ready to use, or for up to 3 days. Purée can be made ahead of time, taking advantage of fruit in season, and frozen for future use. If storing for future use, add 10 percent sugar by weight to help control ice-crystal growth and to maintain a smooth, blended consistency. Just remember that a future recipe's sugar content may need to be adjusted to account for the additional sweetness of the fruit purée. Purée will hold in the freezer for up to 6 months at least, if stored in an airtight container. Defrost frozen purée in the refrigerator before use.

> **TIP ›** The seeds of blueberries, and strawberries are so small they are barely noticeable, and the straining process is potentially maddening. Imagine trying to strain strawberry purée through a mesh so fine that the purée would be allowed through but not the tiny seeds! However, inclusion of these seeds in the final product is a personal choice, depending on the desired texture one is trying to achieve.

MAKING FRUIT COMPOTE

Cooking down fruit into a compote is a technique to consider when using fruit with a high water content. By reducing the water content of the fruit, its natural flavor becomes concentrated. However, this can also impart a "cooked" taste to the finished gelato or sorbet.

To cook down fruit, peel and core it as necessary, then slice or cube it into small pieces. Add a small portion of the sugar (as given in the gelato recipe) to the fruit, mix gently to combine, and let sit overnight. Maceration allows the fruit to release its own juices and provides a nicely flavored cooking liquid.

Place the pieces of fruit and juice in a small to medium-size saucepan (one that easily accommodates all the fruit) and place over low heat. Cook the fruit at a low simmer until it has reached a thick, jam-like consistency. At this point, adding a tiny amount of lemon juice (a squeeze or two, depending on the amount of concentrated fruit rendered) brightens the flavor a bit. A little lemon juice goes a long way, so add one small squeeze, mix it in, and taste it. If the flavor of the fruit could still use a little something, add another squeeze. Be careful not to overdo the lemon or the flavor will become too acidic.

TEMPERING EGG YOLKS

Tempering egg yolks simply means raising the temperature of the cold yolks closer to the temperature of the hot liquid with which they are going to be combined, thereby stabilizing their protein structure and allowing them to thicken the custard base without turning into scrambled eggs.

Separate the yolks from the whites and reserve the whites for another use. Place the yolks in a nonreactive mixing bowl and whisk them slightly to break them up, until they are a homogenous yellow mass. Add a small portion of the sugar (as listed in the gelato recipe) and whisk until the yolks have lightened in color to a pale yellow and have thickened.

Whisk the yolk mixture continuously as the hot liquid is slowly added, one ladleful at a time. Continue to add the hot liquid in this manner until half to most of the hot liquid has been added. The mix should be smooth and creamy.

TIP › When adding sugar to the egg yolks, whisk them together immediately until they are light and thick. Do not add sugar and allow it to sit in the eggs unmixed; this will create small lumps of "cooked" egg yolk in the gelato mix and potentially in the finished product.

TEMPERING EGG YOLKS

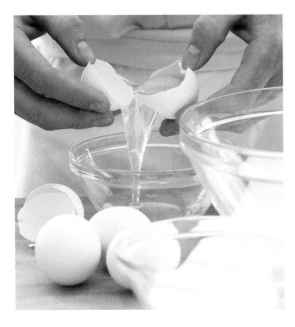

Separate the yolks from the whites and place the yolks in a nonreactive mixing bowl.

Whisk eggs slightly to break them up.

Add a small portion of the sugar called for in the recipe to the eggs.

Whisk the yolk mixture continuously while slowly adding the hot liquid, one ladleful at a time.

Pour the heated egg mixture into the saucepan with the remaining hot liquid and return to the stove top.

Stirring continuously, cook the mixture until thick.

The custard is fully cooked when it reaches 185°F (85°C)

The custard should be thick enough to coat the back of a spoon. A line drawn through the custard will hold its shape.

MAKING A CUSTARD BASE

Pour the heated and tempered egg mixture into the saucepan with the remaining hot liquid and return to the stove top. If using a candy thermometer, insert it now. Whisking continuously, cook over medium to medium-high heat until thick, making sure the mixture does not boil. It's imperative to control the temperature of the cooking custard. If necessary, cook the mixture for a longer time at a lower temperature to ensure the mixture does not overheat or become scorched. If using an instant-read thermometer, insert it now. The custard is ready when it reaches 185°F (85°C). The custard is fully cooked when it is thick enough to coat the back of the spoon or spatula. Another way to test this is to dip the mixing end of the spoon or spatula in the cooked liquid custard and hold it horizontally over the pot. Run your finger across the back of the spoon, drawing a line through the mixture. If the liquid does not instantly cover the line, it is ready. Immediately remove from the heat.

TEMPERING EGG YOLKS

Egg yolks are tempered with hot liquid slowly so that they don't scramble. If the yolks do scramble while making the custard base, it is best to start over. A significant amount of scrambled egg, even if strained out, could impart a cooked-egg taste that, generally, is considered undesirable.

No matter how carefully the custard was crafted, always strain the cooked custard base before using it. Pour the hot liquid through a fine-mesh sieve or strainer and into a clean bowl placed over an ice bath unless otherwise specified in the recipe. The ice bath will allow the hot custard to cool down quickly and immediately stop it from cooking further.

Pour the hot liquid through a fine-mesh sieve or strainer and into a clean bowl.

MAKING SIMPLE SYRUP

Place an equal measured or weighed amount of sugar and water in a small- or medium-size heavy-bottomed saucepan. (The size of the saucepan used is determined by the volume of sugar syrup being made.) Whisk and cook to a boil over medium-high heat. Remove from the heat, whisk briefly. Allow to cool completely. This will ensure that all of the sugar has melted and combined fully with the water. Stored in a clean, airtight container in the refrigerator, it will keep for a couple of weeks.

EMULSIFYING THE GELATO OR SORBET MIX

Emulsifying the gelato mix while it is still hot is recommended. The heat aids in melting the fat molecules so they are more easily dispersed in the liquid, resulting in a better overall texture. Emulsifying ensures that everything is combined, lightening the mix by whipping some air into it before it is frozen.

Although emulsifying can be accomplished with a hand whisk or with a stand blender, a stick or immersion blender is more practical. To emulsify, insert the blade into the hot mixture and blend until smooth.

A slightly imperfect custard can generally be saved by this step (although this technique is not recommended for custard with completely cooked egg in it, which should be discarded).

CHILLING AND AGING THE GELATO OR SORBET MIX

Aging the mix simply means letting the finished mix sit in the refrigerator for at least four hours, or up to overnight. It is the final recommended step of gelato making more than it is a true technique. Gelato mix is aged because the heating (pasteurization) and homogenization process change the physical nature of the mix. When making the mix—before freezing—the heating and cooling process alters the molecular structure of the ingredients. Aging disperses the fat that was melted during the heating process. Additionally, aging assists with the hydration of the sugar. Allowing the mix to rest anywhere from 4 to 16 hours stabilizes it, allowing the sugar to absorb as much water as possible, creating a better overall texture and increasing storage life. The more stable a homemade mix is before it is frozen in a home ice-cream maker, the better the gelato or sorbet will be.

HARDENING THE GELATO OR SORBET

Homemade gelato is best served immediately after removing it from the ice-cream maker. However, if the gelato is to be served at a later time, it must be hardened to establish its proper texture and to control the size of the ice-crystal growth. Although the gelato has just been removed from the ice-cream maker, only about 50 percent of the water is actually frozen. The goal of hardening the gelato is to freeze the remaining water as quickly as possible. The faster the gelato or sorbet is fully frozen, the less time the ice crystals have to grow, resulting in a smoother product.

Hardening is more of a recommended step than an actual technique and is simple to do. Once the mix has been in the ice-cream maker for the specified amount of time, remove the finished gelato or sorbet and place in a well-chilled shallow dish, preferably plastic. Cover with plastic wrap, pressing the wrap gently against the top of the gelato or sorbet, and place in the freezer to fully harden before serving.

REFREEZING WOES

If fresh gelato is placed in a serving dish and sits out while people eat, and the leftovers are then frozen, the gelato is not going to be as good the second time around. The melting and refreezing process causes large ice crystals to form in the gelato, which creates an unpleasant mouthfeel.

CHILLING AND HARDENING THE GELATO
OR SORBET

The gelato mix is poured into the ice-cream maker.

The partially frozen gelato is shown in the ice-cream maker.

Gelato that has not properly hardened after being removed from the ice-cream maker will appear soft.

Gelato that has properly hardened will appear firm and stable.

Use a sharp knife to chop chocolate on a perfectly clean, smooth cutting board for best results.

CHOPPING CHOCOLATE

Use a serrated knife or sharp chef's knife to chop chocolate, starting at the corner of the block and moving inward. If chopping chocolate on a wooden cutting board, make sure that the board has been washed with soap and completely dried since its last use. The cutting board needs to be perfectly clean so that the chocolate doesn't pick up any residual flavors left on the board.

ROASTING NUTS

Most nuts can be roasted in a preheated 350°F (180°C, or gas mark 4) oven, spread out in a single layer on a baking sheet. If using a convection oven that does not automatically adjust the temperature, set the temperature at 325°F (170°C, or gas mark 3). Nuts require about 10 minutes of roasting time, although time may vary depending on the nut and the position of the baking sheet. (Higher in the oven is hotter and will take less time; lower will be cooler.) Nuts with a higher oil content, such as pecans and walnuts, will roast more quickly than other nuts. Stir or toss the nuts once or twice while they are in the oven to ensure an even roast. Monitor the roasting closely: nuts can go from perfectly roasted to burned and inedible in the blink of an eye. Well-roasted nuts should be evenly golden brown on the inside as well as the outside.

REMOVING SEEDS FROM A VANILLA BEAN

Place the vanilla bean flat on a cutting board. Use the tip of a knife to slice the bean in half lengthwise. Run the blade of the knife down the length of the bean, from one end to the other, scraping out the seeds from inside the bean.

Slice the vanilla bean in half lengthwise.

Scrape out the seeds from the sliced vanilla bean.

CHAPTER FIVE
flavor pairings

Good flavor depends on finding a balance among sweet, salty, sour, and bitter. Two ingredients that seemingly would never go together can be combined to produce an unexpectedly good outcome. To some degree, knowing what flavors combine well with others is second nature. If you have been exposed to many different foods and cooking styles, you have a wider repertoire of flavors to draw from when experimenting on your own. Generating unique flavor combinations should be seen as a creative and fun undertaking. While there are no set rules for how to do this, what follows are a few concepts to keep in mind when thinking about taste and flavor.

Flavor is how our brains identify and translate food, and it is dictated by taste. Individual foods are composed of multiple tastes which are transmitted to the brain via thousands of taste buds located on the tongue and roof of the mouth. The brain identifies these sensory messages and attributes a flavor to the food being eaten.

Within a food, one taste usually predominates. Generally, tastes are broken down into four basic categories recognized by taste buds in the mouth: sweet, salty, sour, and bitter. The salty and sweet taste buds are located near the front of the tongue, which is why you instantly know when a dish lacks salt or why licking an ice cream cone is so enjoyable. The sour taste buds line the sides and edges of the tongue. If you have trouble identifying these, suck on a lemon or eat a tart candy and pay attention to the very slight and involuntary clenching of your jaw as the tartness of the lemon juice or the dissolving candy spreads across your tongue. Bitter-perceiving taste buds are found at the very back of your tongue, which is why bitter flavors emerge last and tend to linger.

Sweet and Savory Combinations

Here's one way of looking at this: gelato is a dairy-based foodstuff, and just about anything—sweet, savory, and so on—can be paired with a dairy product to improve it. I'm thinking of everything from fettucine with porcini mushrooms to anchovies in a creamy Caesar dressing. A core philosophy is to start thinking beyond sweet and feel free to personalize the flavors! That's the greatest part, in my opinion, about cooking. You can start with a recipe from just about anywhere, and through changing a couple of things, come up with something completely different, unique, and entirely your own! Recipes are truly jumping-off points for creating new dishes.

If combining flavors isn't something that comes naturally to you, a place to begin can be simply to start reading cookbooks almost as if they're novels. Recipes in a cookbook are not in the same category as Shakespeare, but they can be interesting and, quite informative. Pay attention to how ingredients are used together and to the role that each ingredient plays in a specific dish. Over time, you will intuitively understand flavor pairings and combinations on a more detailed level.

Oftentimes, a savory flavor pairing that works beautifully in an entrée can be transferred to a dessert. One neat place to see this is in the accompaniments to the main element of an entrée—the flavors combined in the sauce, the spices that work well together, and so on.

Lastly, another place to get some great ideas is by looking at restaurant dessert menus. The next time you're out to eat somewhere, take a look at the dessert menu and observe how the flavors are paired together. The chances are quite good that you could use the same types of flavors in a gelato.

UMAMI

Umami is the fifth element of taste and was discovered by a Japanese scientist in the early twentieth century. It is a savory taste that occurs naturally in certain foods and is said to expand and round out flavors. Umami can be found in tomatoes, meat, fish, seaweed, and many dairy products, just to name a few.

Pairings for Gelato and Sorbet Flavors

Below are some common and not-so-common flavor combinations that work well together within gelato and sorbet recipes—or in any dish.

CHOCOLATE: coffee, cinnamon, vanilla, Earl Grey tea, pistachios, hazelnuts, mint, orange

COFFEE: hazelnut, vanilla, cinnamon, lemon, chocolate

APPLE: caramel, brown sugar, ginger, cinnamon, cloves, nutmeg, rum, coriander, honey, maple syrup

BANANA: peanut butter, rum, chocolate, coconut, lime, honey, ginger, blueberries, bacon, vanilla

BLUEBERRIES: lemon, vanilla, cinnamon, maple syrup, sour cream, thyme, ginger

BLACKBERRIES/RASPBERRIES: red wine, orange, honey, cinnamon, almonds, chocolate, brandy

CANTALOUPE AND OTHER MELONS: ginger, lemongrass, lime, port, vanilla, strawberries, cucumber, basil

MANGO: coconut, passion fruit, rum, star anise, black pepper, cloves, blackberries

GRAPEFRUIT: honey, rum, coriander, rosemary, soft cheeses, brown sugar

FIGS: walnuts, caramel, honey, Marsala, lavender, ginger, coconut, cinnamon, mint, port, raspberries, black pepper

STRAWBERRIES: balsamic vinegar, bananas, almonds, lemon, mascarpone cheese, coconut, cream cheese, orange, pink peppercorn, rhubarb, light red wines, zabaglione, maple syrup

recipes

These recipes are some of my all-time favorites, some tried-and-true classic flavors, and some new creations. Where appropriate, I have added options for variations, although you should feel free to also experiment on your own.

Included in this section are recipes for gelati, sorbetti, and granitas. Gelati are dairy based and therefore denser in body and heavier on the palate. Sorbets are made from a sugar-syrup base and traditionally feature fruit flavors. I have also added some more nontraditional sorbet flavors for a nice variety.

Granitas are the simplest of the frozen treats, and these recipes can give you a good foundation to proceed to the sorbet and gelato recipes.

CHAPTER SIX

gelato

Just as all executive chefs, pastry chefs, and chocolatiers add their own personality to their culinary creations, so do gelato makers to their gelato. Although the basic ingredients of gelato don't vary much, the length of time one gelato maker cooks the custard, churns the base, or combines flavoring agents creates infinite nuances in the finished product.

Once you sample a few of these recipes, you will notice that most follow a basic order of techniques. These are the same techniques used by professional gelato makers, and techniques I learned in my years of study and practice. With enough practice and experimentation, you will likely come up with some subtle recipe changes of your own, enjoying the fruits of your labors along the way.

peach gelato

To maximize the flavor of this gelato, it should be made at the height of summer, when peaches are ripest and in season. The sweetness of the peaches combined with the fullness of the cream is a classic flavor combination that is hard to beat. Make this once and it will become a perennial favorite!

FOR THE PEACH PURÉE:

2 cups (300 grams) fresh peaches, peeled, pitted, and cubed, 3 tablespoons (39 g) granulated sugar

2½ teaspoons (12.5 ml) freshly squeezed lemon juice, strained

FOR THE MACERATED PEACHES:

1 cup (122 grams) fresh peaches peeled, pitted, and diced

3 tablespoons (39 g) granulated sugar

FOR THE GELATO:

1¾ cups (410 ml) whole milk

¾ cup (150 g) granulated sugar

4 large egg yolks

3 tablespoons (60 g) all-natural peach jam, optional

1 cup (240 ml) heavy cream

½ teaspoon (2.5 ml) pure vanilla extract

½ cup (115 g) sour cream

1 cup (250 grams) homemade or store-bought peach purée

To make the peach purée: Place the cubed peaches in a medium-size, nonreactive bowl with the sugar and lemon juice. Mix gently to combine and allow the peaches to macerate for ½ hour, covered, in the refrigerator. Once macerated, place all in a blender and purée until smooth. Set aside until ready to use up to 1 day if placed in an airtight container and stored in the refrigerator. Because peach purée will oxidize, press plastic wrap tight against the surface of the purée until ready to use.

To make the macerated peaches: Combine the diced peaches and sugar in a small, nonreactive bowl and toss gently until the peaches are fully coated in sugar. Cover and chill 2 hours while gelato is processing in the ice-cream freezer. Before adding the macerated peaches to the gelato, drain off the syrup and discard.

To make the gelato: Place the milk and all but ¼ cup (50 g) of the sugar in a medium-size, heavy-bottomed saucepan over medium heat and cook, stirring occasionally, until it registers 170°F (77°C) on an instant-read thermometer.

In a nonreactive, medium-size bowl, whisk together the egg yolks and remaining ¼ cup (50 g) of sugar until foamy and slightly thickened.

Carefully temper the egg yolks (see page 64) with the hot milk mixture by slowly adding about half of the hot liquid to the eggs, whisking continuously. Whisk the heated egg mixture into the saucepan with the hot milk, add the peach jam if desired, mix to combine, and return to the stove top. Stirring continuously with a wooden spoon or heatproof rubber spatula, cook the mixture over medium heat until it registers 185°F (85°C) on an instant-read thermometer or is thick enough to coat the back of the spoon or spatula, taking care to make sure the mixture does not boil. Remove from the heat, and using either a stick blender or a regular blender, emulsify the mix (see page 68), if not completely smooth, before incorporating into the cold cream.

Pour the heavy cream into a clean, large stainless-steel or glass mixing bowl set over an ice bath (see page 67).

Pour the heated custard through a fine-mesh sieve or strainer into the cold cream, add the vanilla extract and sour cream, and stir until fully incorporated. Add the peach purée to the strained custard. Stir occasionally (about every 5 minutes or so) until the mixture has fully cooled. This should take about ½ hour. Remove the mixing bowl from the ice bath, dry off the bottom of the bowl if necessary, cover with plastic wrap, and chill in the refrigerator for at least 8 hours or overnight.

When ready, pour the chilled mixture into the ice-cream maker and process according to manufacturer's specifications. When the gelato is about 2 minutes from being done, slowly add the macerated peach pieces. Finish processing the gelato.

Remove the finished gelato from the ice-cream maker and place in a plastic container. Cover with plastic wrap by pressing the wrap gently against the top of the gelato, affix lid to container, and place in the freezer to fully harden before serving.

Yield: approximately 1 quart (528 g)

raspberry gelato

Tangy yet sweet, this vibrantly colored gelato is most delicious when raspberries are in season late spring to early fall. Although traditionally made with red raspberries, black raspberries or golden raspberries can also be used. (Mixing varieties, however, may result in a gelato with an unappealing hue!)

{EASY}

1¾ cups (410 ml) whole milk

1¼ cups (295 ml) heavy cream

2 tablespoons (40 g) all-natural raspberry jam

1 cup plus 2 tablespoons (226 grams) granulated sugar

4 large egg yolks

2 teaspoons (10 ml) freshly squeezed lemon juice, strained

1 cup (232 grams) raspberry purée, strained (see page 63), from 3 cups (330 grams) fresh (best) or frozen raspberries

Pour the milk, ¼ cup (60 ml) of the cream, raspberry jam, and ¾ cup plus 2 tablespoons (175 g) of the sugar into a medium-size, heavy-bottomed saucepan and place over medium heat. Heat, stirring occasionally, until the mixture registers 170°F (77°C) on an instant-read thermometer.

In a nonreactive, medium-size bowl, whisk together the egg yolks and remaining ¼ cup (50 g) of sugar until foamy and slightly thickened.

Carefully temper the egg yolks (see page 64) with the hot mixture by slowly adding about half of the hot liquid to the eggs, whisking continuously. Whisk the heated egg mixture into the saucepan and return to the stove top. Stirring continuously with a wooden spoon or heatproof rubber spatula, cook the mixture over medium heat until it registers 185°F (85°C) on an instant-read thermometer or is thick enough to coat the back of the spoon or spatula, taking care to make sure the mixture does not boil. Remove from the heat. Emulsify the mix (see page 68), if not completely smooth, before incorporating it into the cold cream.

In a nonreactive, medium-size bowl, whisk together the lemon juice and the raspberry purée.

Pour the heated custard through a fine-mesh sieve or strainer into a large, clean mixing bowl set over an ice bath (see page 67). While whisking, add the combined lemon juice and purée and whisk until fully incorporated. Stir occasionally (about every 5 minutes or so) until the mixture has fully cooled. This should take about ½ hour.

Remove the mixing bowl from the ice bath, dry off the bottom of the bowl if necessary, cover with plastic wrap and chill in the refrigerator for at least 8 hours or overnight.

When ready, pour the chilled mixture into the ice-cream maker and process according to manufacturer's specifications. Remove the finished gelato from the ice-cream maker and place in a plastic container. Cover with plastic wrap by pressing the wrap gently against the top of the gelato, affix lid to container, and place in the freezer to fully harden before serving.

Yield: approximately 1 quart (528 g)

VARIATIONS

Raspberry Almond › Add 1 tablespoon (15 ml) almond liqueur, such as amaretto, after the gelato mix has cooled and before it is placed in the refrigerator.

Raspberry Chocolate › Carefully shave a piece of dark chocolate with a serrated knife to yield approximately 2 to 3 ounces (55 to 85 g). Add the chocolate shavings to the ice-cream maker about 2 minutes prior to removing the gelato.

strawberry gelato

If you were looking for a reason to go strawberry pick-ing, here it is. Strawberry gelato is almost as wonderful to look at and to smell as it is to eat. Almost. As a frozen treat, gelato elevates strawberries and cream beyond a mere complementary flavor pairing. As with most fruit recipes, this one is best served when strawberries are in season and at their ripest. Macerating the strawberries before adding them to the gelato will also help to bring out their full flavor and sweetness.

{EASY}

FOR THE STRAWBERRY PURÉE:

2 cups (365 grams) fresh strawberries, rinsed and hulled

1½ tablespoons (20 g) granulated sugar

2 teaspoons (10 ml) freshly squeezed lemon juice

FOR THE MACERATED STRAWBERRIES:

1 cup (160 grams) fresh strawberries, rinsed, hulled, and quartered

3 tablespoons (39 g) granulated sugar

FOR THE GELATO:

1¾ cups (410 ml) whole milk

¾ cup (150 g) granulated sugar

4 large egg yolks

2 tablespoons (40 g) all-natural strawberry jam, optional

1¼ cups (295 ml) heavy cream

1 cups (250 ml) homemade or store-bought strawberry purée

To make the strawberry purée: Cut the berries in half and place in a medium-size, nonreactive bowl with the 1½ tablespoons (20 g) of sugar. Mix gently to combine and allow the berries to macerate several hours, covered in the refrigerator. Once macerated, place in a blender and purée until smooth. Stir in the lemon juice and set aside until ready to use or for up to 2 days in an airtight container in the refrigerator.

To make the macerated strawberries: Combine the strawberries and sugar in a small, nonreactive bowl and toss gently until the berries are fully coated in sugar. Cover and chill several hours in the refrigerator and until ready to use. Before adding the macerated berries to the gelato, drain off the syrup and discard.

To make the gelato: Place the milk and approximately ½ cup (100 g) of the sugar in a medium-size, heavy-bottomed saucepan over medium heat and cook, stirring occasionally, until the mixture registers 170°F (77°C) on an instant-read thermometer.

In a nonreactive, medium-size bowl, whisk together the egg yolks and remaining ¼ cup (50 g) of the sugar until foamy and slightly thickened.

Carefully temper the egg yolks (see page 64) with the hot milk mixture by slowly adding about half of the hot liquid to the eggs, whisking continuously. Whisk the heated egg mixture into the saucepan with the hot milk, add the strawberry jam if desired, mix to combine, and return to the stove top. Stirring continuously with a wooden spoon or heatproof rubber spatula, cook the mixture over medium heat until it registers 185°F (85°C) on an instant-read thermometer or is thick enough to coat the back of the spoon or spatula, taking care to make sure the mixture does not boil. Remove from the heat. Emulsify the mix (see page 68), if not completely smooth, before incorporating it into the cold cream.

Pour the heavy cream into a clean, large stainless-steel or glass mixing bowl set over an ice bath (see page 67).

Pour the heated custard through a fine-mesh sieve or strainer into the cold cream and stir until fully incorporated. Add the strawberry purée to the strained custard. Stir occasionally (about every 5 minutes) until the mixture has fully cooled. This should take about ½ hour. Remove the mixing bowl from the ice bath, dry off the bottom of the bowl if necessary, cover with plastic wrap, and chill in the refrigerator for at least 8 hours or overnight.

When ready, pour the chilled mixture into the ice-cream maker and process according to manufacturer's specifications. When the gelato is about 2 minutes from being done, slowly add the strawberry pieces. Finish processing the gelato.

Remove the finished gelato from the ice-cream maker and place in a plastic container. Cover with plastic wrap by pressing the wrap gently against the top of the gelato, affix lid to container, and place in the freezer to fully harden before serving.

Yield: approximately 1 quart (528 g)

french vanilla gelato

Rich in mouthfeel, this recipe celebrates the best of basic gelato ingredients: milk, cream, eggs, and sugar. If you prefer a stronger vanilla flavor, add the seeds of a second vanilla bean. Or, to vary the distinctive vanilla flavor characteristics, use vanilla beans of different origins (Tahitian, or Mexican) each time you make this recipe.

1 vanilla bean, preferably Madagascar Bourbon

2 cups (475 ml) whole milk

¾ cup (150 g) granulated sugar

4 large egg yolks

1 cup (240 ml) heavy cream

¾ teaspoon (3.75 ml) pure vanilla extract

Split vanilla bean in half with a knife and remove seeds (see page 69). Place the seeds and vanilla bean pod in a medium-size, heavy-bottomed saucepan. Add the milk and ½ cup (100 g) of the sugar. Stir to combine. Place over medium heat and cook, stirring occasionally, until the mixture registers 170°F (77°C) on an instant-read thermometer. Remove from the heat, cover, and let steep for ½ hour.

Remove the vanilla bean pod and place the steeped mixture back on the stove top over medium heat. Warm, stirring occasionally to keep the bottom from scorching, until it registers 170°F (77°C) on an instant-read thermometer.

In a nonreactive, medium-size bowl, whisk together the egg yolks and remaining ¼ cup (50 g) of sugar until foamy and slightly thickened.

Carefully temper the egg yolks (see page 64) with the hot milk mixture by slowly adding about half of the hot liquid to the eggs, whisking continuously. Whisk the heated egg mixture into the saucepan with the hot milk and return to the stove top. Stirring continuously with a wooden spoon or heatproof rubber spatula, cook the mixture over medium heat until it registers 185°F (85°C) on an instant-read thermometer or is thick enough to coat the back of the spoon or spatula, making sure the mixture does not boil. Remove from the heat and emulsify the mix (see page 68), if not completely smooth, before incorporating it into the cold cream.

Pour the heavy cream into a clean, large stainless-steel or glass mixing bowl set over an ice bath (see page 67).

Pour the heated custard through a fine-mesh sieve or strainer into the cold cream, add the vanilla extract, and stir until fully incorporated. Stir occasionally (about every 5 minutes or so) until the mixture has fully cooled. This should take about ½ hour. Remove the mixing bowl from the ice bath, dry off the bottom of the bowl if necessary, cover with plastic wrap, and chill in the refrigerator for at least 8 hours or overnight.

When ready, pour the chilled mixture into the ice-cream maker and process according to manufacturer's specifications.

Remove the finished gelato from the ice-cream maker and place in a plastic container. Cover with plastic wrap by pressing the wrap gently against the top of the gelato, affix lid to container, and place in the freezer to fully harden before serving.

Yield: approximately 1 quart (528 g)

madagascar bourbon vanilla gelato

1 vanilla bean, preferably Madagascar Bourbon

1¹⁄₂ cup (355 ml) whole milk

³⁄₄ cup (150 g) granulated sugar

1¹⁄₂ cups (360 ml) heavy cream

³⁄₄ teaspoon (3.75 ml) pure vanilla extract

This style of gelato is closer to a traditional Philadelphia-style ice cream than an actual gelato. The lack of egg yolks creates a "cleaner" dairy flavor that permits the subtle nuances between different types of vanilla to come through. The fat usually provided by the egg yolks is instead contributed by the heavy cream.

Split the vanilla bean in half with a knife and remove the seeds (see page 67). Place seeds and vanilla bean pod in a medium-size, heavy-bottomed saucepan and add the milk and ³⁄₄ cup (150 g) of sugar. Stir to combine. Place over medium heat and cook, stirring occasionally, until the mixture registers 170°F (77°C) on an instant-read thermometer. Remove from the heat, cover, and let steep for ¹⁄₂ hour.

Remove the vanilla bean pod, add the cream and the vanilla extract, and stir until fully incorporated. Pour into a clean container, cover with plastic wrap, and chill in the refrigerator for at least 8 hours or overnight.

When ready, pour the chilled mixture into the ice-cream maker and process according to manufacturer's specifications.

Remove the finished gelato from the ice-cream maker and place in a plastic container. Cover with plastic wrap by pressing the wrap gently against the top of the gelato, affix lid to container, and place in the freezer to fully harden before serving.

Yield: approximately 1 quart (528 g)

pistachio gelato

Every gelateria in Italy offers this classic flavor. Whether it is made with pistachio paste or fresh nuts will determine the amount of pistachio flavor and the color of the gelato. When using fresh nuts, unsalted will better control the amount of salt in the finished product. If unsalted pistachios cannot be found, buy salted, shell them, and rinse them under cold water for about 1 minute. Allow them to dry completely before roasting them in the oven.

Lightly roast the whole pistachios in the oven as directed on page 71. Roughly chop ¼ cup (35 grams) of the pistachios and reserve to stir into the gelato at the end.

3 cups (710 ml) whole milk, plus additional as needed

1½ cups (220 grams) whole, unsalted, raw pistachios, shelled and lightly roasted

Pinch of salt

¾ cup (150 g) granulated sugar

4 large egg yolks

1 cup (240 ml) heavy cream

¼ teaspoon (1.25 ml) pure vanilla extract

¼ cup (35 g) pistachios, chopped

Pour the milk into a medium-size, heavy-bottomed saucepan, place over medium heat, and cook until almost boiling, approximately 190°F (88°C) on an instant-read thermometer. Add the 1½ cups (220 grams) of whole roasted nuts and allow to simmer for 15 minutes. Remove from the heat and let sit, covered, for 1 hour, stirring occasionally.

Working in batches, process the heated mixture on high speed in a blender or food processor until almost smooth, with only some very small nut pieces remaining. Pour into a clean, medium-size bowl and allow to sit, covered, for 1 hour at room temperature.

When ready, pour the mixture into a medium-size bowl through a fine-mesh strainer or a double layer of cheesecloth. Use a wooden spoon or spatula to press against the nutmeat while straining to remove as much of the nut-infused milk as possible. Measure 2 cups (473 ml) of nut-infused milk, adding plain milk if necessary to equal 2 cups (473 ml) total. Transfer the nut-infused milk to a heavy-bottomed saucepan.

Place the saucepan over medium heat, add the salt and all but ¼ cup (50 g) of the sugar, and heat until the mixture registers 170°F (77°C) on an instant-read thermometer.

In a nonreactive, medium-size bowl, whisk together the egg yolks and remaining ¼ cup (50 g) of sugar until foamy and slightly thickened. Carefully temper the egg yolks (see page 64) with the hot milk mixture by slowly adding about half of the hot liquid to the eggs, whisking continuously. Whisk the heated egg mixture into the saucepan with the hot milk and return to the stove top. Stirring continuously with a wooden spoon or heatproof rubber spatula, cook the mixture over medium-low heat until it registers 185°F (85°C) on an instant-read thermometer or is thick enough to coat the back of the spoon or spatula, making sure the mixture does not boil. Remove from the heat and carefully emulsify the mix (see page 68) if not completely smooth, before incorporating it into the cold cream.

Pour the heated custard through a fine-mesh sieve or strainer into the Irish cream, add the vanilla extract, and stir until fully incorporated. Stir occasionally (about every 5 minutes or so) until the mixture has fully cooled. This should take about ½ hour. Remove the mixing bowl from the ice bath, dry off the bottom of the bowl if necessary, cover with plastic wrap, and chill in the refrigerator for at least 8 hours or overnight.

When ready, pour the chilled mixture into the ice-cream maker and process according to manufacturer's specifications. When the gelato is about 2 minutes from being done, add the chopped pistachios.

Remove the finished gelato from the ice-cream maker and place in a plastic container. Cover with plastic wrap by pressing the wrap gently against the top of the gelato, affix lid to container, and place in the freezer to fully harden before serving.

Yield: approximately 1 quart (528 g)

irish cream gelato

It's hard to put a finger on what about Irish cream is so enticing. It may be the way the chocolate and caramel flavors come together so nicely with the Irish whisky and the smooth cream. Luckily, it makes a great gelato too! This flavor is a perennial favorite in our store, and I think it translates equally well to the home freezer.

2 cups (475 ml) whole milk

½ cup (120 ml) heavy cream

⅔ cup (133 g) granulated sugar

2 teaspoons (2.7 g) arrowroot or cornstarch

4 large egg yolks

½ cup (120 ml) Irish cream liquor

¼ teaspoon (1.25 ml) pure vanilla extract

Pour the milk and cream into a medium-size, heavy-bottomed saucepan. Add ⅓ cup (66g) of the sugar, place over medium heat, and cook, stirring occasionally, until the mixture registers 170°F (77°C) on an instant-read thermometer.

In a nonreactive, medium-size bowl, whisk together the remaining sugar and starch until well combined. The starch should be evenly dispersed in the sugar. Add the egg yolks and whisk until foamy and slightly thickened.

Carefully temper the egg yolks (see page 64) with the hot milk mixture by slowly adding about half of the hot liquid to the eggs, whisking continuously. Whisk the heated egg mixture into the saucepan with the hot milk and return to the stove top. Stirring continuously with a wooden spoon or heatproof rubber spatula, cook the mixture over medium heat until it registers 185°F (85°C) on an instant-read thermometer or is thick enough to coat the back of the spoon or spatula, taking care to make sure the mixture does not boil. Remove from the heat. Emulsify the mix (see page 68), if not completely smooth, before incorporating it into the cold cream.

Pour the Irish cream into a clean, large stainless-steel or glass mixing bowl set over an ice bath (see page 67).

Pour the heated custard through a fine-mesh sieve or strainer into the Irish cream, add the vanilla extract, and stir until fully incorporated. Stir occasionally (about every 5 minutes or so) until the mixture has fully cooled. This should take about ½ hour. Remove the mixing bowl from the ice bath, dry off the bottom of the bowl if necessary, cover with plastic wrap, and chill in the refrigerator for at least 8 hours or overnight. When ready, pour the chilled mixture into the ice-cream maker and process according to manufacturer's specifications.

Remove the finished gelato from the ice-cream maker and place in a plastic container. Cover with plastic wrap by pressing the wrap gently against the top of the gelato, affix lid to container, and place in the freezer to fully harden before serving.

Yield: approximately 1 quart (528 g)

honey and toasted sesame seed gelato

Honey is a wonderful ingredient in that it adds sweetness to a recipe as well as imparts a lovely flavor. Numerous varietal or artisanal honeys are available on the market today. Experiment with several to see which one your palate prefers.

If you are unable to find toasted sesame in the store, don't despair. Sesame seeds are easily toasted in the same manner as roasting nuts (see page 71). However, keep a watchful eye on them, as they burn easily.

2 cups (475 ml) whole milk

⅓ cup (115 g) strong-flavored honey (darker in color)

4 large egg yolks

¼ cup (50 g) granulated sugar

1 cup (240 ml) heavy cream

1 teaspoon (5 ml) toasted sesame oil

1½ teaspoons (4 g) toasted sesame seeds

TIP › An alternative to oven roasting is to place the sesame seeds in a clean, dry skillet over medium heat. Stir with a spoon or heatproof spatula. Let rest for about 30 seconds, stir, let rest for another 30 seconds, stir, and so on, until the seeds begin to turn golden brown. Be very careful, at the moment they start to brown, the seeds will go from perfect to burned in the blink of an eye.

Place the milk and honey in a medium-size, heavy-bottomed saucepan and stir to combine. Place over medium heat and cook, stirring occasionally, until the mixture registers 170°F (77°C) on an instant-read thermometer.

In a nonreactive, medium-size bowl, whisk together the egg yolks and sugar until foamy and slightly thickened.

Carefully temper the egg yolks (see page 64) with the hot milk mixture by slowly adding about half of the hot liquid to the eggs, whisking continuously. Whisk the heated egg mixture into the saucepan with the hot milk and return to the stove top. Stirring continuously with a wooden spoon or heatproof rubber spatula, cook the mixture over medium heat until it registers 185°F (85°C) on an instant-read thermometer or is thick enough to coat the back of the spoon or spatula, taking care to make sure the mixture does not boil. Remove from the heat. Emulsify the mix (see page 68), if not completely smooth, before incorporating into the cold cream.

Pour the heavy cream into a clean, large stainless-steel mixing bowl or glass set over an ice bath (see page 67).

Pour the heated custard through a fine-mesh sieve or strainer into the cold cream, add the sesame oil and seeds, and stir until fully incorporated. Stir occasionally (about every 5 minutes or so) until the mixture has fully cooled. This should take about ½ hour. Remove the mixing bowl from the ice bath, dry off the bottom of the bowl if necessary, cover with plastic wrap, and chill in the refrigerator for at least 8 hours or overnight.

When ready, pour the chilled mixture into the ice-cream maker and process according to manufacturer's specifications.

Remove the finished gelato from the ice-cream maker and place in a plastic container. Cover with plastic wrap by pressing the wrap gently against the top of the gelato, affix lid to container, and place in the freezer to fully harden before serving.

Yield: approximately 1 quart (528 g)

lemon-poppy seed gelato

A good friend's love of lemon-poppyseed muffins inspired this flavor. I created this recipe using gelato instead of lemon sorbet, as the creaminess of the gelato is a better conductor for the flavor of the poppy seeds. Additionally, the crunchy poppy seeds provide a nice contrast to the creamy texture of the gelato.

Zest of 2 large lemons

¾ cup (150 g) granulated sugar

2 cups (475 ml) whole milk

1 cup (240 ml) heavy cream

Peel of 1 lemon, finely shredded and pith-free

4 large egg yolks

2 teaspoons (3.6 g) poppy seeds

Place the lemon zest and sugar into the bowl of a food processor and pulse until fully incorporated. The mixture may be slightly clumpy due to the moisture from the lemon zest.

Pour 1 cup (240 ml) of the milk, the cream, and the lemon peel into a medium-size, heavy-bottomed saucepan. Add ½ cup (100 g) of the lemon sugar mixture, reserving ¼ cup (50 g) of sugar.

Place over medium heat and cook, stirring occasionally, until the mixture registers 170°F (77°C) on an instant-read thermometer. Remove from heat, cover, and let steep for ½ hour.

Strain the mixture through a fine-mesh sieve (to remove lemon peel) into a clean, medium-size, heavy-bottomed saucepan. Place over medium heat and warm, stirring occasionally to keep the bottom from scorching, until it registers 170°F (77°C) on an instant-read thermometer.

In a nonreactive, medium-size bowl, whisk together the egg yolks and remaining ¼ cup (50 g) of the lemon sugar until foamy and slightly thickened.

Carefully temper the egg yolks (see page 64) with the hot milk mixture by slowly adding about half of the hot liquid to the eggs, whisking continuously. Whisk the heated egg mixture into the saucepan with the hot milk and return to the stove top. Stirring continuously with a wooden spoon or heatproof rubber spatula, cook the mixture over medium heat until it registers 185°F (85°C) on an instant-read thermometer or is thick enough to coat the back of the spoon or spatula, taking care to make sure the mixture does not boil. Remove from the heat. Emulsify the mix (see page 68), if not completely smooth, before incorporating it into the cold cream.

Pour the remaining 1 cup (240 ml) milk into a clean, large stainless-steel or glass mixing bowl set over an ice bath (see page 67).

Pour the heated custard through a fine-mesh sieve or strainer into the cold milk and stir until fully incorporated. Stir occasionally (about every 5 minutes or so) until the mixture has fully cooled. This should take about ½ hour. Remove the mixing bowl from the ice bath, dry off the bottom of the bowl if necessary, cover with plastic wrap, and chill in the refrigerator for at least 8 hours or overnight.

When ready, pour the chilled mixture into the ice-cream maker and process according to manufacturer's specifications. When the gelato is about 2 minutes from being done, slowly add the poppy seeds. Finish processing the gelato.

Remove the finished gelato from the ice-cream maker and place in a plastic container. Cover with plastic wrap by pressing the wrap gently against the top of the gelato, affix lid to container, and place in the freezer to fully harden before serving.

Yield: approximately 1 quart (528 g)

blueberry lavender gelato

The origins of this novel flavor combination have long escaped from memory. Regardless of how it was dreamed up, the sweetness of the blueberries and the floral notes of the lavender marry beautifully to create a unique and utterly addicting flavor combination.

1¾ (410 ml) cups whole milk

1¼ cups (295 ml) heavy cream, divided

2 teaspoons (2 g) organic dried lavender buds (see note)

3 tablespoons (60 g) all-natural blueberry jam
1 cup (200 g) granulated sugar

4 large egg yolks
2 teaspoons (10 ml) freshly squeezed lemon juice, strained

1 cup (about 330 g) blueberry purée, from 3 cups of fresh (best) or frozen blueberries (See page 63.)

Place the milk, ¼ cup (60 ml) cream, and lavender buds into a medium saucepan and heat just until boiling. Remove from heat, cover, and let steep 15 minutes. Pour through a strainer into a 2-cup (475 ml) liquid measure to remove the lavender buds, pressing on the buds to remove as much liquid as possible. Add cream as necessary to make sure you have 2 cups (475 ml) of liquid after you have strained out the lavender buds. Place the lavender milk and ¾ cup sugar into a medium-size, heavy-bottomed saucepan and place over medium heat. Heat, stirring occasionally, until the mixture registers 170°F (77°C) on instant-read thermometer.

In a non-reactive, medium-size bowl, whisk together the egg yolks and the remaining sugar until foamy.

Carefully temper the egg yolks (see page 64) with the hot mixture by slowly adding about half of the hot liquid to the eggs, whisking continuously. Whisk the heated egg mixture into the saucepan with the hot milk and cream, add the blueberry jam, mix to combine, and return to the stove top. Stirring continuously with a wooden spoon or heatproof rubber spatula, cook the mixture over medium heat until it registers 185°F (85°C) on an instant-read thermometer, or is thick enough to coat the back of the spoon or spatula, taking care to make sure the mixture does not boil. Remove from the heat. Emulsify the mix (see page 68) if not completely smooth.

In a separate non-reactive, medium-size bowl, whisk together the lemon juice and the blueberry purée.

Pour the heated custard through a fine-mesh sieve or strainer into a large, clean mixing bowl set over an ice bath (see page 67). While whisking, add the combined lemon juice and purée and stir until fully incorporated. Continue stirring occasionally (about every 5 minutes or so) until the mixture has fully cooled. This should take about half an hour. Remove the mixing bowl from the ice bath, dry off the bottom of the bowl if necessary, cover with plastic wrap and chill in the refrigerator for at least 8 hours or overnight.

When ready, pour the chilled mixture into the ice-cream maker and process according to manufacturer's specifications.

Remove the finished gelato from the ice-cream maker and place in a plastic container. Cover with plastic wrap by pressing the wrap gently against the top of the gelato, affix lid to container, and place in the freezer to fully harden before serving.

Yield: 1 quart (528 g)

Note: Lavender buds are generally available at health food and natural grocery stores.

chocolate gelato

True chocoholics can use chocolate with a higher percentage of cocoa. Likewise, if your tastes run toward the milder side, substitute milk chocolate with a lower percentage of cocoa in place of the bittersweet.

Pour the milk into a medium-size, heavy-bottomed saucepan. Whisk the cocoa powder and ¾ cup (150 g) of the sugar together in a small bowl and whisk into the cold milk in the saucepan. Place over medium heat and heat the milk until an instant-read thermometer reads between 180°F and 190°F (82°F and 88°C). Continue to heat and cook at this temperature for 5 minutes, stirring constantly.

{MEDIUM}

2 cups (475 ml) whole milk

2 tablespoons plus 1 teaspoon (14 g) unsweetened, Dutch-processed cocoa powder

Pinch of salt

6 ounces (170 g) bittersweet chocolate, finely chopped

4 large egg yolks

1 cup (200 g) granulated sugar

1 cup (240 ml) heavy cream

¾ teaspoon (3.75 ml) pure vanilla extract

Remove from the heat, whisk in chopped bittersweet chocolate, and stir until all of the chocolate has completely melted. In a nonreactive, medium-size bowl, whisk together the egg yolks, the remaining ¼ cup (50 g) of sugar, and salt until foamy and slightly thickened.

Carefully temper the egg yolks (see page 64) with the milk mixture by slowly adding about half of the hot liquid to the eggs, whisking continuously. Whisk the heated egg mixture into the hot milk and return to the stove top. Stirring continuously with a wooden spoon or heatproof rubber spatula, cook the mixture over medium heat until it registers 185°F (85°C) on an instant-read thermometer, or is thick enough to coat the back of the spoon or spatula, taking care to make sure the mixture does not boil. Remove from the heat. Emulsify the mix (see page 68), if not completely smooth, before incorporating it into the cold cream.

Pour the heavy cream into a clean, large stainless-steel or glass mixing bowl set over an ice bath (see page 67).

Pour the heated chocolate custard through a fine-mesh sieve or strainer into the cold cream, add the vanilla extract, and stir until fully incorporated. Stir occasionally (about every 5 minutes or so) until the mixture has fully cooled. This should take about ½ hour. Remove the mixing bowl from the ice bath, dry off the bottom of the bowl if necessary, cover with plastic wrap, and chill in the refrigerator for at least 8 hours or overnight.

When ready, pour the chilled mixture into the ice-cream maker and process according to manufacturer's specifications.

Remove the finished gelato from the ice-cream maker and place in a plastic container. Cover with plastic wrap by pressing the wrap gently against the top of the gelato, affix lid to container, and place in the freezer to fully harden before serving.

Yield: approximately 1 quart (528 g)

VARIATIONS

Chocolate-Vanilla Gelato › Vanilla adds lighter floral/fruity notes to the chocolate. Split a vanilla bean in half lengthwise and scrape the seeds into the milk, adding the pod as well. Heat to a simmer. Remove from the heat, then cover and steep for 15 to 20 minutes. Remove the vanilla pod, and follow the Chocolate Gelato recipe from step 1.

Fudgy Brownie Gelato › Begin with either store-bought brownies or brownies baked from scratch. Lay the brownies on a baking sheet and place in the freezer. When frozen, remove and let thaw for 15 to 20 minutes. Carefully use a sharp knife to cut the brownies into small dice. (Freezing reduces the amount of crumbs created in this step.) Stir in 1 cup (150 g) or more chopped brownie pieces into the gelato right as it is finishing in the ice-cream maker, generally about 2 minutes before it is done. Allow the gelato to harden in the freezer before serving as indicated.

espresso gelato

Espresso, like gelato, is quintessentially Italian. Therefore, it seemed a natural progression to create an espresso-flavored gelato. In the summer, I will often have a scoop of espresso gelato after dinner instead of a steaming hot espresso. And in the winter, I sometimes add a scoop to my hot chocolate for more of a mocha experience. The flavor of this gelato depends on the coffee beans, so the quality and freshness of the beans is paramount.

{MEDIUM}

2¾ cups (650 ml) whole milk, plus additional as needed

1 cup (70 grams) dark-roasted coffee beans

1 cup (200 g) granulated sugar

4 large egg yolks

1 cup (235 ml) heavy cream

¼ teaspoon (1.25 ml) pure vanilla extract

Pour milk into a medium-size, heavy-bottomed saucepan, place over medium heat, and cook, stirring occasionally, until the milk registers 190°F (88°C) on an instant-read thermometer. Remove from the heat, add the coffee beans, and allow to steep, covered, for 15 minutes.

Working in batches if necessary, process the heated mixture on medium speed in a blender or food processor until the mixture becomes a medium brown or tan color—like coffee with cream added to it.

Pour into a clean, medium-size bowl and allow to sit, covered, for 15 minutes at room temperature. Strain mixture through a fine-mesh sieve into a clean container and, if necessary, add in enough milk until amount of liquid equals 2 cups (475 ml).

Pour the milk mixture into a medium-size saucepan and place over medium heat. Add ¾ cup (150 g) of the sugar and warm, stirring occasionally to keep the bottom from scorching, until it registers 170°F (77°C) on an instant-read thermometer.

In a nonreactive, medium-size bowl, whisk together the egg yolks and the remaining ¼ cup (50 g) of the sugar until foamy and slightly thickened.

Carefully temper the egg yolks (see page 64) with the hot milk mixture by slowly adding about half of the hot liquid to the eggs, whisking continuously. Pour the heated egg mixture into the saucepan with the hot milk and return to the stove top. Stirring continuously with a wooden spoon or heatproof rubber spatula, cook the mixture over medium heat until it registers 185°F (85°C) on an instant-read thermometer or is thick enough to coat the back of the spoon or spatula, taking care to make sure the mixture does not boil. Remove from the heat and strain into a blender through a fine-mesh sieve to remove any coffee-bean bits. Emulsify the mix (see page 68), if not completely smooth, before incorporating it into the cold cream.

Pour the heavy cream into a clean, large stainless steel or glass mixing bowl set over an ice bath (see page 67).

Pour the strained and puréed custard into the cold cream, add the vanilla extract, and stir until fully incorporated. Stir occasionally (about every 5 minutes or so) until the mixture has fully cooled. This should take about ½ hour.

Remove the mixing bowl from the ice bath, dry off the bottom of the bowl if necessary, cover with plastic wrap, and chill in the refrigerator for at least 8 hours or overnight.

When ready, pour the chilled mixture into the ice-cream maker and process according to manufacturer's specifications.

Remove the finished gelato from the ice-cream maker and place in a plastic container. Cover with plastic wrap by pressing the wrap gently against the top of the gelato, affix lid to container, and place in the freezer to fully harden before serving.

Yield: approximately 1 quart (528 g)

macadamia nut gelato

I originally created this gelato for a local chef who loves macadamia-nut cookies and was looking for a frozen alternative to use in his desserts. If macadamias are hard to find or not to your liking, you could substitute another nut such as a cashew or Brazil nut, each of which is similar to macadamias in texture and fat content.

{MEDIUM}

3 cups (710 ml) whole milk, plus additional as needed

2 cups (290 grams) raw macadamia nuts, shelled and roughly chopped

Pinch of salt

4 large egg yolks

¾ cup (150 g) granulated sugar

1 cup (240 ml) heavy cream

¼ teaspoon (1.25 ml) pure vanilla extract

Pour the milk into a medium-size, heavy-bottomed saucepan, place over medium heat, and cook, stirring occasionally, until it registers 190°F (88°C) on an instant-read thermometer. Add 1¾ cups (255 g) of the nuts and allow to barely simmer for 10 minutes. Remove from the heat and let sit, covered, for 15 minutes, stirring occasionally.

Working in batches, process the heated mixture in a blender or food processor until completely smooth. Let mixture sit 1 hour. If visible pieces of nuts remain, you will need to strain the mixture before proceeding. To do this, pour the mixture into a clean mixing bowl through a fine-mesh strainer or a double-layer of cheesecloth. Use a wooden spoon or spatula to press against any remaining nutmeat inside the strainer or cheesecloth to remove as much of the nut-infused milk as possible. Measure out into a clean container and, if necessary, add enough milk until amount of liquid equals 2 full cups (475 ml). Pour into a medium-size saucepan, add the salt, ½ cup (100 g) of the sugar and place over medium-high heat. Warm, stirring occasionally to keep the bottom from scorching, until it registers 170°F (77°C) on an instant-read thermometer.

In a nonreactive, medium-size bowl, whisk together the egg yolks and the remaining ¼ cup (50 g) of the sugar until foamy and slightly thickened.

Carefully temper the egg yolks (see page 64) with the hot milk mixture by slowly adding about half of the hot liquid to the eggs, whisking continuously. Whisk the heated egg mixture into the saucepan with the hot milk and return to the stovetop. Stirring continuously with a wooden spoon or heatproof rubber spatula, cook the mixture over medium heat until it registers 185°F (85°C) on an instant-read thermometer or is thick enough to coat the back of the spoon or spatula, taking care to make sure the mixture does not boil. Remove from the heat. Emulsify the mix (see page 68), if not completely smooth, before incorporating it into the cold cream.

Pour the heavy cream into a clean, large stainless steel or glass mixing bowl set over an ice bath (see page 67).

Pour the heated custard through a fine-mesh sieve or strainer into the cold cream, add the vanilla extract, and stir until fully incorporated. Stir occasionally (about every 5 minutes or so) until the mixture has fully cooled. This should take about ½ hour. Remove the mixing bowl from the ice bath, dry off the bottom of the bowl if necessary, cover with plastic wrap, and chill in the refrigerator for at least 8 hours or overnight.

When ready, pour the chilled mixture into the ice-cream maker and process according to manufacturer's specifications. When the gelato is about 2 minutes from being done, slowly add the remaining chopped nuts. Finish processing the gelato.

Remove the finished gelato from the ice-cream maker and place in a plastic container. Cover with plastic wrap by pressing the wrap gently against the top of the gelato, affix lid to container, and place in the freezer to fully harden before serving.

Yield: approximately 1 quart (528 g)

cookies and cream gelato

I would be remiss if I did not include a recipe for this flavor. It is the most popular gelato sold in my store and is a flavor found in virtually every ice-cream shop. Inspired by its popular cookie counterpart, the combination is one that is hard to beat: crunchy chocolate cookies and rich vanilla creaminess.

{MEDIUM}

2 cups (470 ml) whole milk

¾ cup (150 g) granulated sugar

4 large egg yolks

1 cup (235 ml) heavy cream

½ teaspoon (2.5 ml) pure vanilla extract

5 chocolate sandwich cookies, chopped medium-fine

Pour the milk into a medium-size, heavy-bottomed saucepan and add ½ cup (100 g) of the sugar.. Stir to combine. Place over medium heat and cook, stirring occasionally, until it registers 170°F (77°C) on an instant-read thermometer.

In a nonreactive, medium-size bowl, whisk together the egg yolks and the remaining ¼ cup (50 g) of the sugar until foamy and slightly thickened.

Carefully temper the egg yolks (see page 64) with the hot milk mixture by slowly adding about half of the hot liquid to the eggs, whisking continuously. Pour the heated egg mixture into the saucepan with the hot milk and return to the stove top. Stirring continuously with a wooden spoon or heatproof rubber spatula, cook the mixture over medium heat until it registers 185°F (85°C) on an instant-read thermometer or is thick enough to coat the back of the spoon or spatula, taking care to make sure the mixture does not boil. Remove from the heat. Emulsify the mix (see page 68), if not completely smooth, before incorporating it into the cold cream.

Pour the heavy cream into a clean, large stainless-steel or glass mixing bowl set over an ice bath (see page 67).

Pour the heated custard through a fine-mesh sieve or strainer into the cold cream, add the vanilla extract, and stir until fully incorporated. Stir occasionally (about every 5 minutes or so) until the mixture has fully cooled. This should take about ½ hour. Remove the mixing bowl from the ice bath, dry off the bottom of the bowl if necessary, cover with plastic wrap, and chill in the refrigerator for at least 8 hours or overnight.

Three to 4 hours before processing the chilled mixture in the ice-cream maker, place the chopped cookie pieces on a parchment paper–lined baking sheet in the freezer until fully frozen and ready to use.

When ready, pour the chilled mixture into the ice-cream maker and process according to manufacturer's specifications.

Remove the finished gelato from the ice-cream maker, stir in chopped frozen cookies, and place in a plastic container. Cover with plastic wrap by pressing the wrap gently against the top of the gelato, affix lid to container, and place in the freezer to fully harden before serving.

Yield: approximately 1 quart (528 g)

stracciatella

Stracciatella means "little rags" and refers to small chocolate bits reminiscent of torn-up strips of cloth. This gelato is the Italian version of American-style chocolate chip ice cream. If making the stracciatella sauce is too labor intensive, replace it with the best-quality store-bought miniature chocolate chips.

FOR THE GELATO:

2 cups (475 ml) whole milk

¾ cups (150 g) granulated sugar

4 large egg yolks

1 cup (240 ml) heavy cream

¼ teaspoon (1.25 ml) pure vanilla extract

FOR THE STRACCIATELLA SAUCE:

4 ounces (115 g) dark chocolate, finely chopped

1 teaspoon (5 ml) coconut (preferred) or other neutral vegetable oil

To make the gelato: Place the milk and ½ cup (100 g) of the sugar in a medium-size, heavy-bottomed saucepan and stir to combine. Place over medium heat and cook, stirring occasionally, until the milk registers 170°F (77°C) on an instant-read thermometer.

In a nonreactive, medium-size bowl, whisk together the egg yolks and remaining ¼ cup (50 g) of sugar until foamy and slightly thickened.

Carefully temper the egg yolks (see page 64) with the hot milk mixture by slowly adding about half of the hot liquid to the eggs, whisking continuously. Pour the heated egg mixture into the saucepan with the hot milk and return to the stove top. Stirring continuously with a wooden spoon or heatproof rubber spatula, cook the mixture over medium heat until it registers 185°F (85°C) on an instant-read thermometer or is thick enough to coat the back of the spoon or spatula, making sure the mixture does not boil. Remove from the heat. Emulsify the mix (see page 68), if not completely smooth, before incorporating it into the cold cream.

Pour the heavy cream into a clean, large stainless-steel or glass mixing bowl set over an ice bath (see page 67).

Pour the heated custard through a fine-mesh sieve or strainer into the cold cream, add the vanilla extract, and stir until fully incorporated. Stir occasionally (about every 5 minutes or so) until the mixture has fully cooled. This should take about ½ hour. Remove the mixing bowl from the ice bath, dry off the bottom of the bowl if necessary, cover with plastic wrap, and chill in the refrigerator for at least 8 hours or overnight.

When ready, pour the chilled mixture into the ice-cream maker and process according to manufacturer's specifications. When the gelato is about 2 minutes from being done, slowly drizzle in the stracciatella sauce. The sauce should be warm and liquid but not hot. Finish processing the gelato.

Remove the finished gelato from the ice-cream maker and place in a plastic container. Cover with plastic wrap by pressing the wrap gently against the top of the gelato, affix lid to container, and place in the freezer to fully harden before serving.

To make the stracciatella sauce: Combine the chocolate and oil in a small, microwave-safe bowl and place in the microwave oven. Melt on medium heat for about 1 minute, depending on the power of your microwave. Keep an eye on the melting chocolate as you don't want to overheat it and cause it to burn. Remove from the microwave every 20 to 30 seconds and stir. Remove completely when fully melted and smooth. Allow to cool slightly before adding into the processing gelato in the ice-cream maker as directed in the recipe. (The sauce can also be prepared in a double boiler on the stove top.)

Yield: approximately 1 quart (528 g)

mint chip gelato

Mint and chocolate is a timeless, delicious flavor combination. The flavor of the gelato base depends entirely on the strength and freshness of the mint and the amount used. If the amount of mint called for is not to your liking, you can increase or decrease that amount as desired. Likewise, if milk chocolate is your preferred chocolate, substitute that for the dark. There is usually room to adjust a recipe according to your personal tastes as long as you are careful and choose your substitutions wisely.

2 cups (480 ml) whole milk

¾ cup (150 g) granulated sugar

2 cups (lightly packed) fresh mint leaves, cleaned and patted dry

4 large egg yolks

1 cup (240 ml) heavy cream

¼ teaspoon (1.25 ml) pure vanilla extract

½ cup (90 grams) chopped dark chocolate

> **TIP ›** For a stronger mint taste and a more vibrant color, reserve ½ cup (100 g) of the mint leaves before steeping for the first time. After making the custard, add the reserved mint leaves and emulsify thoroughly, leaving bits of mint in the mix. If an even stronger taste is desired, add an additional ¼ teaspoon (1.25 ml) of pure mint extract.

Pour the milk into a medium-size, heavy-bottomed saucepan. Add approximately ½ cup (100 g) of the sugar, place over medium heat, and cook, stirring occasionally, until the mixture registers 170°F (77°C) on an instant-read thermometer. Remove from the heat, add the mint leaves, and stir to make sure that they're fully submerged (don't worry if they float to the top). Cover and let steep for 2 hours. (The longer the mint leaves steep, the stronger the mint flavor will be.)

Strain through a fine-mesh sieve into a clean, medium-size, heavy-bottomed saucepan, pressing on the mint leaves to remove as much flavor as possible. Discard the mint leaves and place the steeped mixture back on the stove top over medium heat. Warm, stirring occasionally to keep the bottom from scorching, until it registers 170°F (77°C) on an instant-read thermometer.

In a nonreactive, medium-size bowl, whisk together the egg yolks and remaining ¼ cup (50 g) of sugar until foamy and slightly thickened.

Carefully temper the egg yolks (see page 64) with the hot milk mixture by slowly adding about half of the hot liquid to the eggs, whisking continuously. Pour the heated egg mixture into the saucepan with the hot milk and return to the stove top. Stirring continuously with a wooden spoon or heatproof rubber spatula, cook the mixture over medium heat until it registers 185°F (85°C) on an instant-read thermometer or is thick enough to coat the back of the spoon or spatula, taking care to make sure the mixture does not boil. Remove from the heat. Emulsify the mix (see page 68), if not completely smooth, before incorporating it into the cold cream.

Pour the heavy cream into a clean, large stainless-steel or glass mixing bowl set over an ice bath (see page 67).

Pour the heated custard through a fine-mesh sieve or strainer into the cold cream, add the vanilla extract, and stir until fully incorporated. Stir occasionally (about every 5 minutes) until the mixture has fully cooled. This should take about ½ hour. Remove the mixing bowl from the ice bath, dry off the bottom of the bowl if necessary, cover with plastic wrap, and chill in the refrigerator for at least 8 hours or overnight.

When ready, pour the chilled mixture into the ice-cream maker and process according to manufacturer's specifications. When the gelato is about 2 minutes from being done, slowly add the chopped chocolate. Finish processing the gelato.

Remove the finished gelato from the ice-cream maker and place in a plastic container. Cover with plastic wrap by pressing the wrap gently against the top of the gelato, affix lid to container, and place in the freezer to fully harden before serving.

Yield: approximately 1 quart (528 g)

milk chocolate chunk

Made with both cocoa powder and milk chocolate, this gelato recipe offers rich flavor without overwhelming the palate. For a more intense chocolate experience, choose dark chocolate instead of milk chocolate. For a smooth texture, omit the final addition of chocolate completely.

2 cups (475 ml) whole milk

2 tablespoons plus 1 teaspoon (14 g) unsweetened, Dutch-processed cocoa powder

1 cup (200 g) granulated sugar

6 ounces (170 g) milk chocolate, finely chopped

4 large eggs yolks

Pinch of salt

1 cup (240 ml) heavy cream

¾ teaspoon (3.75 ml) pure vanilla extract, optional

½ cup (88 grams) chopped milk chocolate

Pour the milk into a medium-size, heavy-bottomed saucepan. Whisk the cocoa powder and ¾ cup (150 g) of the sugar together in a small bowl and whisk into the cold milk in the saucepan. Place over medium heat until an instant-read thermometer reads between 180°F and 190°F (82°F and 88°C). Continue to heat and cook at this temperature for 5 minutes, stirring constantly.

Remove from the heat, let cool 5 minutes, whisk in the finely chopped milk chocolate, and stir until all of the chocolate has completely melted.

In a nonreactive, medium-size bowl, whisk together the egg yolks, the remaining ¼ cup (50 g) of sugar, and salt until foamy and slightly thickened.

Carefully temper the egg yolks (see page 64) with the hot chocolate milk by slowly adding about half of the hot liquid to the eggs, whisking continuously. Whisk the heated egg mixture into the saucepan with the hot milk and return to the stove top. Stirring continuously with a wooden spoon or heatproof rubber spatula, cook the mixture over medium heat until it registers 185°F (85°C) on an instant-read thermometer or is thick enough to coat the back of the spoon or spatula, taking care to make sure the mixture does not boil. Remove from the heat. Emulsify the mix (see page 68), if not completely smooth, before incorporating it into the cold cream.

Pour the heavy cream into a clean, large stainless-steel or glass mixing bowl set over an ice bath (see page 67).

Pour the heated chocolate custard through a fine-mesh sieve or strainer into the cold cream, add the vanilla extract, and stir until fully incorporated. Stir occasionally (about every 5 minutes or so) until the mixture has fully cooled. This should take about ½ hour. Remove the mixing bowl from the ice bath, dry off the bottom of the bowl if necessary, cover with plastic wrap, and chill in the refrigerator for at least 8 hours or overnight.

When ready, pour the chilled mixture into the ice-cream maker and process according to manufacturer's specifications. When the gelato is about 2 minutes from being done, slowly add the chopped chocolate. Finish processing the gelato.

Remove the finished gelato from the ice-cream maker and place in a plastic container. Cover with plastic wrap by pressing the wrap gently against the top of the gelato, affix lid to container, and place in the freezer to fully harden before serving.

Yield: approximately 1 quart (528 g)

hot chocolate gelato

My first attempt at this gelato was a disaster. The combination of chile peppers resulted in such an intense heat on the palate that I only sold one serving in my store, to a customer who bought it for her husband out of spite!

This revised version uses only one type of chile and the heat index has been scaled down. Remember, however, that with all chile peppers, it's difficult to assess their potency until tasted. So don't be completely surprised if this recipe is "hotter" at some times than others.

2 cups (475 ml) whole milk

2 large or 3 small dried ancho chiles, whole

2 tablespoons plus 1 teaspoon (14 g) unsweetened, Dutch-processed cocoa powder

4 large egg yolks

1 cup (200 g) granulated sugar

6 ounces (170 g) bittersweet chocolate, finely chopped

Pinch of salt

2 pinches of cayenne pepper, optional

1 cup (240 ml) heavy cream

¾ teaspoon (3.75 ml) pure vanilla extract, optional

Pour the milk into a medium-size heavy-bottomed saucepan, place over medium heat, and cook, stirring occasionally, until it registers 170°F (77°C) on an instant-read thermometer. Remove from the heat, add the dried chiles, cover, and let steep for 45 minutes.

Use a slotted spoon to remove the chiles from the milk. Carefully stem and seed the chiles, discard the stems and seeds, and set the chiles aside until ready to use.

Whisk the cocoa powder and ¾ cup (150 g) of the sugar together in a small bowl and whisk into the chile milk mixture in the saucepan. Return the mixture to the stove top and place over medium heat. Continue to heat, and cook the mixture between 180°F and 190°F (82°F and 88°C) for 5 minutes, stirring constantly.

Remove from the heat, whisk in the chopped bittersweet chocolate, and stir until all of the chocolate has completely melted.

In a nonreactive, medium-size bowl, whisk together the egg yolks, the remaining ¼ cup (50 g) of the sugar, and salt until foamy and slightly thickened.

Carefully temper the egg yolks (see page 64) with the hot chocolate milk by slowly adding about half of the hot liquid to the eggs, whisking continuously. Whisk the heated egg mixture into the saucepan with the hot milk and return to the stove top. Stirring continuously with a wooden spoon or heatproof rubber spatula, cook the mixture over medium heat until it registers 185°F (85°C) on an instant-read thermometer or is thick enough to coat the back of the spoon or spatula, taking care to make sure the mixture does not boil. Remove from the heat.

Pour the custard into a blender and add the seeded chiles and cayenne, if using. Blend on high speed for 30 seconds or until smooth and emulsified.

Pour the heavy cream into a clean, large stainless-steel or glass mixing bowl set over an ice bath (see page 67).

Pour the blended custard through a fine-mesh sieve or strainer into the cold cream, add the vanilla extract if using, and stir until fully incorporated. Stir occasionally (about every 5 minutes) until the mixture has fully cooled. This should take about ½ hour. Remove the mixing bowl from the ice bath, dry off the bottom of the bowl if necessary, cover with plastic wrap, and chill in the refrigerator for at least 8 hours or overnight.

When ready, pour the chilled mixture into the ice-cream maker and process according to manufacturer's specifications.

Remove the finished gelato from the ice-cream maker and place in a plastic container. Cover with plastic wrap by pressing the wrap gently against the top of the gelato, affix lid to container, and place in the freezer to fully harden before serving.

Yield: approximately 1 quart (528 g)

pink peppercorn gelato

Pink peppercorns are somewhat misleading in name as they are more floral and fruity than peppery in essence, which makes them an ideal flavor profile to infuse into cream. I am sure you will be pleasantly surprised when you taste this gelato.

{MEDIUM}

2 cups (475 ml) whole milk

1 cup (240 ml) heavy cream

¾ cup (150 g) granulated sugar

⅛ cup plus 1 tablespoon (15 g) pink peppercorns, lightly crushed

4 large egg yolks

½ teaspoon (2.5 ml) vanilla extract

Place the milk, ¼ cup (60 ml) of the cream, ½ cup (100 g) of the sugar, and crushed peppercorns in a medium-size heavy-bottomed saucepan and stir to combine. Place over medium heat and cook, stirring occasionally, until the mixture registers 190°F (88°C) on an instant-read thermometer. Remove from the heat, cover, and let steep for 1 hour.

Strain the steeped mixture through a fine-mesh sieve (to remove the peppercorns) into a clean, medium-size, heavy-bottomed saucepan. Use a wooden spoon or spatula to press against any remaining peppercorn pieces inside the sieve to remove as much of the flavor as possible. Place strained mixture back on stove top over medium-high heat. Warm, stirring occasionally to keep the bottom from scorching, until it registers 170°F (77°C) on an instant-read thermometer.

In a nonreactive, medium-size bowl, whisk together the egg yolks and the remaining ¼ cup (50 g) of the sugar until foamy and slightly thickened.

Carefully temper the egg yolks (see page 64) with the hot milk mixture by slowly adding about half of the hot liquid to the eggs, whisking continuously. Whisk the heated egg mixture into the saucepan with the hot milk and return to the stove top. Stirring continuously with a wooden spoon or heatproof rubber spatula, cook the mixture over medium heat until it registers 185°F (85°C) on an instant-read thermometer or is thick enough to coat the back of the spoon or spatula, taking care to make sure the mixture does not boil. Remove from the heat and emulsify the mix (see page 68), if not completely smooth, before incorporating it into the cold cream.

Pour the remaining ¾ cup (180 ml) heavy cream into a clean, large stainless-steel or glass mixing bowl set over an ice bath (see page 67).

Pour the heated custard through a fine-mesh sieve or strainer into the cold cream, add the vanilla extract, and stir until fully incorporated. Stir occasionally (about every 5 minutes) or until the mixture has fully cooled. This should take about ½ hour. Remove the mixing bowl from the ice bath, dry off the bottom of the bowl if necessary, cover with plastic wrap, and chill in the refrigerator for at least 8 hours or overnight.

When ready, pour the chilled mixture into the ice-cream maker and process according to manufacturer's specifications.

Remove the finished gelato from the ice-cream maker and place in a plastic container. Cover with plastic wrap by pressing the wrap gently against the top of the gelato, affix lid to container, and place in the freezer to fully harden before serving.

Yield: approximately 1 quart (528 g)

dark chocolate-
orange gelato

Dark chocolate and orange have been linked since chocolate was first discovered and brought to Europe from the New World. In this recipe, the candied orange rind, in addition to providing flavor, imparts some texture into the otherwise smooth gelato.

FOR THE CANDIED ORANGE RIND:

4 large unblemished oranges

6 cups (1200 g) sugar

FOR THE GELATO:

Zest of 2 large or 3 medium oranges

1 cup (200 g) granulated sugar

2 tablespoons plus 1 teaspoon (14 grams) unsweetened, Dutch-processed cocoa powder

2 cups (475 ml) whole milk

6 ounces (170 g) bittersweet chocolate, finely chopped

4 large egg yolks

Pinch of salt

1 cup (240 ml) heavy cream

½ teaspoon (2.5 ml) pure vanilla extract

½ recipe Candied Orange Rind or high-quality purchased candied rind, finely chopped

To make the Candied Orange Rind: Fill three 4-quart (3.8 L) saucepans with water and bring the water to a boil. Cut each orange vertically (through the stem end) into eight wedges. Peel and reserve rind from each wedge.

Trim off the pointed ends of rind wedges, and cut each wedge into strips 1½ to 2 inches long (3.75 to 5 cm) and ¼ inch (0.6 cm) wide. Discard any irregular trimmings.

When the water boils, submerge the strips into one pot, keeping them down with a spoon if necessary. Return the water to a full boil, and then boil the orange rind for 2 minutes. Drain the rind immediately, and then place it in the second pot of boiling water. Return the water to a boil, and boil for 2 minutes. Drain. Place the rind in the third pot of water. Boil for 2 minutes. Drain well.

In another deep saucepot, combine 5 cups (1000 g) sugar and 5 cups (1.2 L) water. Boil over medium heat until the sugar has dissolved. Add the rind to the sugar syrup, making sure it is submerged. Insert a candy thermometer and boil, stirring occasionally, until the thermometer reads 238°F (114°C) degrees. The rinds should be translucent at this point.

Drain the rinds and transfer them to a wire rack placed over a cookie sheet or waxed paper. Allow them to dry in a single layer in a warm, dry place overnight, until barely sticky.

Reserve half of the orange rind and chop into small dice (for the Dark Chocolate Orange recipe). Take the remaining rind and, in a large bowl, toss the rinds with the remaining 1 cup (200 g) of the sugar, to coat evenly. Store in a covered container at room temperature. If the rinds become moist/sticky, toss them in sugar again.

To make the Gelato:
Place the orange zest and 1 cup (200 g) of the sugar into the bowl of a food processor and pulse until fully incorporated. The mixture may be slightly clumpy due to the moisture from the orange zest.

Whisk the cocoa powder and ¾ cup (150 g) of the orange sugar together in a small bowl. Pour the milk into a medium-size, heavy-bottomed saucepan. Whisk in the cocoa powder and sugar mixture until fully incorporated, and place over medium-high heat. Heat the cocoa powder mixture, stirring occasionally, until the mixture reaches 190°F (88°C). Reduce the heat and cook between 180°F and 190°F (82°C and 88°C) for 5 minutes, stirring constantly.

Remove from the heat, whisk in chopped bittersweet chocolate, and stir until all of the chocolate has completely melted.

(continued)

(continued)

In a nonreactive, medium-size bowl, whisk together the egg yolks, the remaining ¼ cup (50 g) of sugar, orange sugar, and salt until foamy and slightly thickened.

Carefully temper the egg yolks (see page 64) with the hot chocolate milk by slowly adding about half of the hot liquid to the eggs, whisking continuously. Whisk the heated egg mixture into the saucepan with the hot milk and return to the stove top. Stirring continuously with a wooden spoon or heatproof rubber spatula, cook the mixture over medium heat until it registers 185°F (85°C) on an instant-read thermometer or is thick enough to coat the back of the spoon or spatula, taking care to make sure the mixture does not boil. Remove from the heat. Emulsify the mix (see page 68), if not completely smooth, before incorporating it into the cold cream.

Pour the heavy cream into a clean, large stainless steel mixing bowl set over an ice bath (see page 67).

Pour the heated chocolate custard through a fine-mesh sieve or strainer into the cold cream, add the vanilla extract, and stir until fully incorporated. Stir occasionally (about every 5 minutes or so) until the mixture has fully cooled. This should take about ½ hour. Remove the mixing bowl from the ice bath, dry off the bottom of the bowl if necessary, cover with plastic wrap, and chill in the refrigerator for at least 8 hours or overnight.

Three to 4 hours before processing the chilled mixture in the ice-cream maker, place the chopped, candied orange rind on parchment paper–lined baking sheet in the freezer until fully frozen and ready to use.

When ready, pour the chilled mixture into the ice-cream maker and process according to manufacturer's specifications. When the gelato is about 2 minutes from being done, slowly add the frozen candied orange rind. Finish processing the gelato.

Remove the finished gelato from the ice-cream maker and place in a plastic container. Cover with plastic wrap by pressing the wrap gently against the top of the gelato, affix lid to container, and place in the freezer to fully harden before serving.

Yield: approximately 1 quart (528 g)

candied ginger gelato

Ginger's natural sharpness is tempered by the process of being cooked in sugar. When making this gelato, you will be left with extra ginger-infused simple syrup. Don't throw it away; the remaining syrup can be used to add a ginger zing to some cocktails or to liven up a fruit salad!

{EASY}

FOR THE CANDIED GINGER:

2-inch (5 cm) piece fresh ginger, peeled and cut into small dice

1½ cups (360 ml) simple syrup (see page 68)

FOR THE GELATO:

1 cup (240 ml) heavy cream

¾ cup (150 g) granulated sugar

1- to 1½-inch (2.5 to 3.75 cm) piece fresh ginger, peeled and finely chopped

2 cups (480 ml) whole milk

4 large egg yolks

To make the candied ginger: Place the ginger and simple syrup in a small, heavy-bottomed saucepan over medium heat and cook until the mixture begins to simmer. Reduce the heat to low and simmer, covered, for 40 minutes, until the ginger is candied and translucent. Use a slotted spoon to remove the ginger from the syrup and set aside until ready to use. If desired, reserve the ginger syrup for another use.

To make the gelato: Place the cream, ½ cup (100 g) of the sugar, and the ginger in a medium-size, heavy-bottomed saucepan. Stir to combine. Place over medium heat and cook, stirring occasionally, until mixture registers 190°F (88°C) on an instant-read thermometer. Remove from heat, cover, and let steep for 1 hour.

Strain the steeped mixture through a fine-mesh sieve (to remove the ginger pieces) into a clean, medium-size, heavy-bottomed saucepan. Use a wooden spoon or spatula to press against any remaining ginger pieces inside the sieve to remove as much of the ginger flavor as possible. Add 1 cup (240 ml) of the milk to the ginger cream and place strained mixture back on the stove top over medium heat. Warm, stirring occasionally to keep the bottom from scorching, until it registers 170°F (77°C) on an instant-read thermometer.

In a nonreactive, medium-size bowl, whisk together the egg yolks and remaining ¼ cup (50 g) of sugar until foamy and slightly thickened.

Carefully temper the egg yolks (see page 64) with the hot milk mixture by slowly adding about half of the hot liquid to the eggs, whisking continuously. Whisk the heated egg mixture into the saucepan with the hot milk and return to the stove top. Stirring continuously with a wooden spoon or heatproof rubber spatula, cook the mixture over medium heat until it registers 185°F (85°C) on an instant-read thermometer or is thick enough to coat the back of the spoon or spatula, taking care to make sure the mixture does not boil. Remove from the heat. Emulsify the mix (see page 68), if not completely smooth, before incorporating it into the cold milk.

Pour the remaining 1 cup (240 ml) milk into a clean, large stainless-steel or glass mixing bowl set over an ice bath (see page 67).

Pour the heated custard through a fine-mesh sieve or strainer into the cold milk and stir until fully incorporated. Stir occasionally (about every 5 minutes or so) until the mixture has fully cooled. This should take about ½ hour. Remove the mixing bowl from the ice bath, dry off the bottom of the bowl if necessary, cover with plastic wrap, and chill in the refrigerator for at least 8 hours or overnight.

When ready, pour the chilled mixture into the ice-cream maker and process according to manufacturer's specifications. When the gelato is about 2 minutes from being done, slowly add in the candied ginger. Finish processing the gelato.

Remove the finished gelato from the ice-cream maker and place in a plastic container. Cover with plastic wrap by pressing the wrap gently against the top of the gelato, affix lid to container, and place in the freezer to fully harden before serving.

Yield: approximately 1 quart (528 g)

roasted peanut and marshmallow crème gelato

This gelato is inspired by the classic peanut-butter-and-marshmallow-crème sandwich beloved by children and adults alike. While not an overly difficult recipe, the process is somewhat long. However, the result is well worth it! If time is in short supply, store-bought marshmallow crème can be used instead of homemade, but the gelato will be somewhat sweeter and have a less pristine consistency.

FOR THE MARSHMALLOW CRÈME:

10 ounces (280 g) marshmallows

2 tablespoons (28 ml) plus 1 teaspoon (5 ml) water

⅔ cup (133 g) sugar

¼ cup (60 ml) milk

2 teaspoons (15 g) light corn syrup

1 teaspoon (5 ml) pure vanilla extract

FOR THE GELATO:

1½ cups (219 g) whole, unsalted, raw peanuts, shelled

3 cups (710 ml) whole milk, plus additional as needed

¾ cup (150 g) granulated sugar

Pinch of salt

4 large egg yolks

1 cup (240 ml) heavy cream

¼ teaspoon (1.25 ml) pure vanilla extract

¼ cup (37 g) unsalted, raw peanuts, shelled and roughly chopped

To make the marshmallow crème: Place the marshmallows in the top part of a double boiler placed over medium-high heat. Cook until the marshmallows have completely melted, stirring until smooth.

Remove the pan from the heat, but leave the double boiler over the water. Combine the water, sugar, milk, and corn syrup in a medium-size saucepan and heat until boiling. Reduce the heat and simmer for 5 minutes.

Pour the sugar mixture over the melted marshmallows and stir to incorporate. Stir in the vanilla extract and cool. The sauce will thicken as it sits.

To make the gelato: Roast the whole peanuts in the oven as directed on page 71 and set aside until ready to use.

Pour milk into a medium-size, heavy-bottomed saucepan, place over medium heat, and cook until almost boiling, approximately 190°F (88°C) on an instant-read thermometer. Add the roasted, whole nuts and allow to simmer for 15 minutes. Remove from the heat and let sit, covered, for 15 minutes, stirring occasionally.

Working in batches, process the heated mixture in a blender or food processor until almost smooth, with some tiny nut pieces remaining. Pour into a clean, medium-size bowl and allow to sit, covered, for 1 hour at room temperature.

When ready, pour the mixture through a fine-mesh strainer or a double layer of cheesecloth into a medium-size bowl. Use a wooden spoon or spatula to press against the nutmeat inside the strainer or cheesecloth to remove as much of the nut-infused milk as possible. Measure the liquid to ensure there are 2 cups (475 ml), adding additional milk as necessary to equal 2 cups (475 ml). Transfer the liquid to a medium-size heavy-bottomed saucepan.

Place the saucepan over medium heat, add ½ cup (100 g) of the sugar and the salt, and heat until mixture registers 170°F (77°C) on an instant-read thermometer.

In a nonreactive, medium-size bowl, whisk together the egg yolks and the remaining ¼ cup (50 g) of sugar until foamy and slightly thickened.

Carefully temper the egg yolks (see page 64) with the hot milk mixture by slowly adding about half of the hot liquid into the eggs, whisking continuously. Pour the heated egg mixture into the saucepan with the hot milk and return to the stovetop. Stirring continuously with a wooden spoon or heatproof rubber spatula, cook the mixture over medium heat until it registers 185°F (85°C) on an instant-read thermometer or is thick enough to coat the back of the spoon or spatula, taking care to make sure the mixture does not boil. Remove from the heat. Emulsify the mix (see page 68), if not completely smooth, before incorporating it into the cold cream.

Pour the heavy cream into a clean, large stainless steel or glass mixing bowl set over an ice bath (see page 67).

Pour the heated custard through a fine-mesh sieve or strainer into the cold cream, add the vanilla extract, and stir until fully incorporated. Stir occasionally (about every 5 minutes or so) until the mixture has fully cooled. This should take about ½ hour. Remove the mixing bowl from the ice bath, dry off the bottom of the bowl if necessary, cover with plastic wrap, and chill in the refrigerator for at least 8 hours or overnight.

When ready, pour the chilled mixture into the ice-cream maker and process according to manufacturer's specifications. When the gelato is about 2 minutes from being done, slowly add the chopped peanuts and the marshmallow crème. Finish processing the gelato.

Remove the finished gelato from the ice-cream maker and place in a plastic container. Cover with plastic wrap by pressing the wrap gently against the top of the gelato, affix lid to container, and place in the freezer to fully harden before serving.

Yield: approximately 1 quart (528 g)

VARIATION

Peanut Butter › Peanut butter may be used instead of fresh nuts, which results in a gelato that is every bit as delectable as the original. In this variation, omit the peanuts completely and create the custard as above. Follow the instructions to make and cook the custard completely. Emulsify the mixture with a stick blender. Add ½ cup (130 g) all-natural crunchy peanut butter to the custard mixture. Blend again until incorporated. Whisk mixture into the cold cream, and continue with the remainder of the recipe.

hazelnut gelato

Hazelnut is a traditional gelato flavor in Europe and one that has gained popularity elsewhere. The addition of fresh hazelnuts adds richness to the finished product in both taste and mouthfeel. Always use the freshest hazelnuts available and be sure to toast them well to bring out their full flavor. Be careful though—nuts that are overtoasted will introduce bitter undertones into the gelato.

1½ cups (220 g) hazelnuts, toasted and skinned (see page 71)

3 cups (710 ml) whole milk, plus additional as needed

¾ cup (150 g) granulated sugar

4 large egg yolks

Pinch of salt

1 cup (240 ml) heavy cream

¼ teaspoon (1.25 ml) pure vanilla extract

Place the hazelnuts in the container of a food processor fitted with the blade attachment or in a heavy-duty blender. Carefully grind the hazelnuts into a fine meal within a pulsing action. The hazelnuts should be finely chopped but not overly processed into a powder. (Overprocessing will cause the nuts to release their natural oils too early and will create a paste.) Place the ground hazelnuts in a clean bowl and set aside until ready to use.

Pour the milk into a medium-size, heavy-bottomed saucepan and place over medium heat.

Heat the milk, stirring occasionally, until it registers 190°F (88°C) on an instant-read thermometer. Add the ground hazelnuts. Simmer over medium-high heat for approximately 15 minutes, stirring occassionaly, and then remove the saucepan from the stove, cover, and let sit for 1 hour.

Pour the milk mixture through a fine-mesh sieve or strainer into a clean medium-size bowl. Use the back of a ladle or a rubber spatula to gently press the nutmeat against the bottom and inside of the strainer to remove as much of the nut-infused milk as possible. Measure the milk mixture to ensure there are 2 cups (475 ml). If there is less than 2 cups (475 ml) of milk, add milk to equal 2 cups (475 ml). Transfer the milk mixture to a heavy-bottomed medium-size saucepan.

Place the saucepan over medium heat. Add ½ cup (100 g) of the sugar and heat the milk, stirring occasionally, until it registers 170°F (77°C) on an instant-read thermometer.

In a nonreactive, medium-size bowl, whisk together the egg yolks, remaining ¼ cup (50 g) of sugar, and salt until foamy and slightly thickened.

Carefully temper the egg yolks (see page 64) with the hot milk mixture by slowly adding about one-half of the hot liquid to the eggs, whisking continuously. Whisk the heated egg mixture into the saucepan with the hot milk and return to the stove top. Stirring continuously with a wooden spoon or heat proof rubber spatula, cook the mixture over medium heat until it registers 185°F (85°C) on an instant-read thermometer or is thick enough to coat the back of the spoon or spatula, taking care to make sure the mixture does not boil. Remove from the heat. Emulsify the mix (see page 68), if not completely smooth, before incorporating it into the cold cream.

Pour the cold heavy cream into a clean, large stainless-steel or glass mixing bowl set over an ice bath (see page 67.)

Pour the hazelnut custard through a fine-mesh sieve or strainer into the cold cream, add the vanilla extract, and stir until fully incorporated. Stir occasionally (about every 5 minutes or so) until the mixture has fully cooled. This should take about ½ hour. Remove the mixing bowl from the ice bath, dry off the bottom of the bowl if necessary, cover with plastic wrap, and chill in the refrigerator for at least 8 hours or overnight.

When ready, pour the chilled mixture into the ice-cream maker and process according to manufacturer's specifications.

Remove the finished gelato from the ice-cream maker and place in a plastic container. Cover with plastic wrap by pressing the wrap gently against the top of the gelato, affix lid to container, and place in the freezer to fully harden before serving.

Yield: approximately 1 quart (528 g)

peanut butter cup gelato

Peanut butter is a staple in many pantries, and when combined with chocolate, it creates an all-time favorite flavor combination.

If you are a fan of commercially produced peanut-butter-and-chocolate confections, try chopping some and stirring them into the gelato at the end, just before removing the gelato from the ice-cream maker.

Roast all the nuts in the oven as directed on page 71 and set aside until ready to use.

Pour the milk into a medium-size, heavy-bottomed saucepan, place over medium heat, and cook until milk the registers 190°F (88°C) on an instant-read thermometer. Add the roasted, whole peanuts and simmer for 5 to 10 minutes. Remove from the heat and let sit, covered, for 15 minutes, stirring occasionally.

1½ cups (219 g) whole, un-salted, raw peanuts, shelled

3 cups (710 ml) whole milk

2 tablespoons plus 1 teaspoon (14 g) unsweetened, Dutch-processed cocoa powder

1 cup (200 g) granulated sugar

6 ounces (170 g) bittersweet chocolate, finely chopped

4 large egg yolks

Pinch of salt

1 cup (240 ml) heavy cream

¾ teaspoon (3.75 ml) pure vanilla extract

½ cup (120 ml) milk chocolate, chopped

¼ cup (37 g) unsalted, raw peanuts, shelled and roughly chopped

TIP › All-natural peanut butter may also be used in this recipe. But, omit the peanuts completely and make a chocolate custard by starting the recipe with the milk, cocoa powder, salt, and ¾ cup (150 g) sugar. Follow the instructions to make and cook the custard completely. Emulsify the custard with a stick blender or in a stand blender, add ½ cup (100 g) peanut butter. Blend again until smooth, and pour into the cold cream as directed. Continue with the remainder of the recipe.

Working in batches, process the heated mixture in a blender or food processor until almost smooth, with some nut pieces remaining. Pour into a clean, medium-size bowl and allow to sit, covered, for 1 hour at room temperature.

When ready, pour the mixture through a fine-mesh strainer or a double-layer of cheesecloth and into a medium-size, heavy-bottomed saucepan. Use a wooden spoon or spatula to press against the nutmeat inside the strainer or cheesecloth to remove as much of the nut-infused milk as possible.

Whisk the cocoa powder and ¾ cup (150 g) of the sugar together in a small bowl, whisking the mixture into the peanut-infused milk in a medium, heavy-bottomed saucepan. Place over medium heat. Continue to heat, and cook the mixture between 180°F and 190°F (82°F and 88°C) for 5 minutes, stirring constantly.

Remove from the heat, whisk in chopped bittersweet chocolate, and stir until all of the chocolate has completely melted. In a nonreactive, medium-size bowl, whisk together the egg yolks, the remaining sugar, and salt until foamy.

Carefully temper the egg yolks (see page 64) with the hot chocolate milk by slowly adding about half of the hot liquid to the eggs, whisking continuously. Whisk the heated egg mixture into the saucepan with the hot milk and return to the stove top. Stirring continuously with a wooden spoon or heatproof rubber spatula, cook the mixture over medium heat until it registers 185°F (85°C) on an instant-read thermometer or is thick enough to coat the back of the spoon or spatula, taking care to make sure the mixture does not boil. Remove from the heat and emulsify the mix (see page 68), if not completely smooth, before incorporating it into the cold cream.

Pour the heavy cream into a clean, large stainless-steel or glass mixing bowl set over an ice bath (see page 67).

Pour the heated chocolate custard through a fine-mesh sieve or strainer into the cold cream, add the vanilla extract, and stir until fully incorporated. Stir occasionally (about every 5 minutes or so) until the mixture has fully cooled. This should take about ½ hour. Remove the mixing bowl from the ice bath, dry off the bottom of the bowl if necessary, cover with plastic wrap, and chill in the refrigerator for at least 8 hours or overnight.

When ready, pour the chilled mixture into the ice-cream maker and process according to manufacturer's specifications. When the gelato is about 2 minutes from being done, slowly add the chopped milk chocolate and chopped peanuts. Finish processing the gelato.

Remove the finished gelato from the ice-cream maker and place in a plastic container. Cover with plastic wrap by pressing the wrap gently against the top of the gelato, affix lid to container, and place in the freezer to fully harden before serving.

Yield: approximately 1 quart (528 g)

caramel gelato

The simple caramel is incorporated into the gelato base. The result, a smooth gelato infused with caramel flavor, is more sophisticated than the gooey, sticky treat recalled from childhood.

When working with hot sugar while making caramel, exercise caution, as it can cause a nasty burn if it makes contact with your skin. You might want to keep an ice bath at hand in case the hot sugar splatters onto your hands. Quickly submerge them into the icy water to limit the degree of the burn.

{DIFFICULT}

FOR THE CARAMEL:

1½ cups (300 g) granulated sugar

½ cup (120 ml) water

2 tablespoons (44 g) light corn syrup

FOR THE GELATO:

2 cups (475 ml) whole milk

1 batch caramel, ground

4 large egg yolks

Pinch of salt

1 cup (240 ml) heavy cream

¾ teaspoon (3.75 ml) pure vanilla extract

To make the caramel: Place the sugar, water, and the corn syrup in a medium-size, heavy-bottomed saucepan and stir together until the mixture resembles wet sand. Place over high heat, bring to a boil, and cook until the sugar turns a light amber color and just begins to smoke (around 350°F [180°C] on a candy thermometer). Remove from the heat and swirl the pan around as the caramel continues to darken to a medium-dark tan color. Immediately and carefully pour the hot caramel onto a Silpat or parchment paper-lined baking sheet. Allow the caramel to cool completely before breaking it up into small pieces with a rolling pin or by hand.

When completely cooled, place broken-up pieces of caramel into the bowl of a food processor and pulse until it has the consistency of coarse sand or kosher salt. Set aside until ready to use.

To make the gelato: Pour the milk into a medium-size, heavy-bottomed saucepan and add the ground caramel. Stir to combine. Place over medium heat and cook, stirring occasionally, until it registers 170°F (77°C) on an instant-read thermometer.

In a nonreactive, medium-size bowl, whisk together the egg yolks and salt until foamy and slightly thickened.

Carefully temper the egg yolks (see page 64) with the hot milk mixture by slowly adding about half of the hot liquid to the eggs, whisking continuously. Pour the heated egg mixture into the saucepan with the hot milk and return to the stove top. Stirring continuously with a wooden spoon or heatproof rubber spatula, cook the mixture over medium heat until it registers 185°F (85°C) on an instant-read thermometer or is thick enough to coat the back of the spoon or spatula, making sure the mixture does not boil. Remove from the heat. Emulsify the mix (see page 68), if not completely smooth, before incorporating it into the cold cream.

Pour the heavy cream into a clean, large stainless-steel or glass mixing bowl set over an ice bath (see page 67).

Pour the heated custard through a fine-mesh sieve or strainer into the cold cream, add the vanilla extract, and stir until fully incorporated. Stir occasionally (about every 5 minutes or so) until the mixture has fully cooled. This should take about ½ hour. Remove the mixing bowl from the ice bath, dry off the bottom of the bowl if necessary, cover with plastic wrap, and chill in the refrigerator for at least 8 hours or overnight. When ready, pour the chilled mixture into the ice-cream maker and process according to manufacturer's specifications.

Remove the finished gelato from the ice-cream maker and place in a plastic container. Cover with plastic wrap by pressing the wrap gently against the top of the gelato, affix lid to container, and place in the freezer to fully harden before serving.

Yield: approximately 1 quart (528 g)

chocolate-cinnamon-basil gelato

At first glance this may seem like a strange combination of flavors, but chocolate, cinnamon, and basil work quite well together. Basil complements chocolate as mint does, while cinnamon adds a touch of spice. Dark chocolate lends a strong flavor background to tie the overall taste experience together. Cinnamon sticks and fresh basil leaves are preferable to ground cinnamon and dried basil flakes, for a fresher, truer flavor.

4 cinnamon sticks

2 cups (475 ml) whole milk

2 tablespoons plus 1 teaspoon (14 g) unsweetened, Dutch-processed cocoa powder

1 cup (200 g) granulated sugar

6 ounces (170 g) bittersweet chocolate, finely chopped

4 large egg yolks

Pinch of salt

1 cup (240 ml) heavy cream

¾ teaspoon (3.75 ml) pure vanilla extract

⅛ to ¼ cup (5 g to 10 g) basil leaves, chiffonade-cut*

Chiffonade is a culinary term for thin strips. To prepare a chiffonade of basil, stack the basil leaves, roll the stack into a tight bundle, then cut the bundle crosswise into thin strips with a paring knife.

Place the cinnamon sticks in a medium-size heavy-bottomed saucepan and add the milk. Place over medium heat and cook, stirring occasionally, until the mixture registers 170°F (77°C) on an instant-read thermometer. Remove from the heat, cover, and let steep for ½ hour.

Remove the cinnamon sticks from the milk. Whisk the cocoa powder and ¾ cup (150 g) of the sugar together in a small bowl, whisking the mixture into the cinnamon-infused milk in the saucepan. Continue to heat and cook between 180°F and 190°F (82°F and 88°C) for 5 minutes, stirring constantly.

Remove from the heat, whisk in the chopped bittersweet chocolate, and stir until all of the chocolate has completely melted.

In a nonreactive, medium-size bowl, whisk together the egg yolks, remaining ¼ cup (50 g) of the sugar, and salt until foamy and slightly thickened.

Carefully temper the egg yolks (see page 64) with the hot chocolate milk by slowly adding about half of the hot liquid to the eggs, whisking continuously. Whisk the heated egg mixture into the saucepan with the hot milk and return to the stove top. Stirring continuously with a wooden spoon or heatproof rubber spatula, cook the mixture over medium heat until it registers 185°F (85°C) on an instant-read thermometer or is thick enough to coat the back of the spoon or spatula, taking care to make sure the mixture does not boil. Remove from the heat. Emulsify the mix (see page 68), if not completely smooth, before incorporating it into the cold cream.

Pour the heavy cream into a clean, large stainless-steel or glass mixing bowl set over an ice bath (see page 67).

Immediately pour the heated chocolate custard through a fine-mesh sieve or strainer into the cold cream, add the vanilla extract and fresh basil, and stir until fully incorporated. Stir occasionally (about every 5 minutes or so) until the mixture has fully cooled. This should take about ½ hour.

Remove the mixing bowl from the ice bath, dry off the bottom of the bowl if necessary, cover with plastic wrap, and chill in the refrigerator for at least 8 hours or overnight.

When ready, pour the mixture into a blender and blend for 15 seconds on medium, or alternatively, use an immersion blender to emulsify for the same amount of time. Strain the mixture through a fine or medium strainer into the ice-cream maker and process according to manufacturer's specifications.

Remove the finished gelato from the ice-cream maker and place in a plastic container. Cover with plastic wrap by pressing the wrap gently against the top of the gelato, affix lid to container, and place in the freezer to fully harden before serving.

Yield: approximately 1 quart (528 g)

CHAPTER SEVEN

sorbets and granitas

Sorbets and granitas are lighter than gelato in both style and texture. Traditionally fruit based, both are dairy-free and therefore somewhat lower in fat. The lack of an underlying cream taste allows the flavoring of sorbet or granita to come through in a cleaner, stronger manner, resulting in a more intensely flavored dessert.

As with the gelato recipes in Chapter Six, the recipes for sorbets and granitas are each based on similar techniques, despite their flavor variations or inclusions. Therefore, once you master the basics of making a sorbet or granita, feel free to try out some of your own concoctions.

pear sorbet with honey and cumin-candied walnuts

For optimal sweetness and a potent pear flavor, use extremely ripe pears. Varieties with a high water content, such as Bartlett pears, will yield better results. To ripen a slightly green pear, place it in a paper bag and leave it in a cool, dark place until ready to use.

FOR THE SORBET:

1¼ cups (295 ml) water

1 cup (200 g) granulated sugar

4 cups ripe pears peeled, cored, and diced (about 2 pounds [905 g])

2 teaspoons (10 ml) freshly squeezed lemon juice, strained

FOR THE CANDIED WALNUTS:

2 cups (240 g) walnut halves

2 tablespoons (28 g) sweet butter

2 tablespoons (40 g) honey

2 teaspoons (10 ml) water

¼ teaspoon (.6 g) ground cumin

½ teaspoon (3 g) salt

> **TIP** › To keep pears from oxidizing after being peeled and before puréeing, submerge them in a bowl of water until ready to use.

To make the sorbet: Place the water and sugar in a medium-size, heavy-bottomed saucepan and place over medium-high heat. Bring the mixture to a boil, stirring occasionally until the sugar fully dissolves, and continue to boil for about 1 minute. Remove from the heat and set aside to cool, at least 1 hour.

Place the diced pears into the container of a stand blender, add the sugar syrup and the lemon juice, and purée until smooth.

Taste the mixture to see if its sweetness is to your liking. If it seems too sweet, add additional freshly squeezed and strained lemon juice in ½ teaspoon (2.5 ml) increments until the desired level of sweetness is achieved.

Pour into a clean container, cover with a lid or plastic wrap, and chill in the refrigerator for at least 8 hours or overnight.

When ready, pour the chilled mixture into the ice-cream maker and process according to manufacturer's specifications.

Remove the finished sorbet from the ice-cream maker and place in a plastic container. Cover with plastic wrap by pressing the wrap gently against the top of the sorbet, affix lid to container, and place in the freezer to fully harden before serving.

To make the candied walnuts: Preheat the oven to 350°F (180°C, or gas mark 4). Roast walnuts in the oven as directed on page 67 and set aside until ready to use.

Melt the butter in a small, heavy-bottomed saucepan over medium-high heat. Add the honey, water, cumin, and salt, stirring to combine. Insert a candy thermometer or use an instant-read thermometer and cook until mixture registers 235°F (113°C) and has reached the soft ball stage.

If using a candy thermometer, remove it from the mixture at this time and add the roasted walnuts, stirring to coat completely with the hot syrup.

Carefully pour the walnut mixture onto a clean baking sheet lined with parchment paper or a silicone baking mat. Working quickly, use a fork to carefully separate any nuts that may be stuck together.

Return the nuts to the hot oven and bake for 12 minutes, until no longer sticky. Remove from the oven and set the baking sheet on a wire rack to cool.

Sprinkle the cooled nuts over the pear sorbet before serving.

Yield: approximately 1½ quarts (900 g)

1 cup (240 ml) water

¾ cup (150 g) granulated sugar

3 tablespoons (60 g) blackberry preserves or jam

1¾ cups (430 g) blackberry purée (from about 2 pounds [905 g] of blackberries, frozen or fresh) see page 63

blackberry sorbet

Sorbet is a perfect vehicle for blackberries' true essence. A scoop of this sorbet paired with vanilla gelato, is a cool treat of differing taste and texture.

Place the water, sugar, and jam in a medium-size, heavy-bottomed saucepan over medium heat. Bring the mixture to a boil while stirring occasionally until the sugar fully dissolves, and continue to boil for about 1 minute. Remove from the heat and set aside to cool, at least 1 hour.

Add the blackberry purée to the cooled syrup and stir well to combine.

Pour into a clean container, cover with a lid or plastic wrap, and chill in the refrigerator for at least 8 hours or overnight.

When ready, pour the chilled mixture into the ice-cream maker and process according to the manufacturer's specifications.

Remove the finished sorbet from the ice-cream maker and place in a plastic container. Cover with plastic wrap by pressing the wrap gently against the top of the sorbet, affix lid to container, and place in the freezer to fully harden before serving.

Yield: approximately 1½ quarts (900 g)

2½ cups (570 ml) unsweetened coconut milk

¾ cup (133 g) granulated sugar

½ cup (120 ml) freshly squeezed lime juice, strained

2 tablespoons (28 ml) dark rum

Zest from 1 lime

lime in the coconut sorbet

This recipe's name is inspired by the title of a popular song, and the lime-coconut combination is just as popular as an icy confection. The coconut flavor is derived from coconut milk, which gives the sorbet a creamy mouthfeel closer to that of gelato. The rum rounds out the overall flavor, but it is easily omitted if this sorbet will be served to children.

Place the coconut milk and sugar in a medium-size, heavy-bottomed saucepan over medium heat. Bring the mixture to a boil while stirring occasionally until the sugar fully dissolves, and continue to boil for about 1 minute. Remove from the heat and set aside to cool, at least 1 hour.

Add the fresh lime juice and rum into the cooled syrup and stir well to combine.

Pour into a clean container, cover with a lid or plastic wrap, and chill in the refrigerator for at least 8 hours or overnight.

When ready, pour the chilled mixture into the ice-cream maker and process according to manufacturer's specifications. When the sorbet is about 5 minutes from being done, slowly add the fresh zest. Finish processing the sorbet.

Remove the finished sorbet from the ice-cream maker and place in a plastic container. Cover with plastic wrap by pressing the wrap gently against the top of the sorbet, affix lid to container, and place in the freezer to fully harden before serving.

Yield: approximately 1½ quarts (900 g)

¾ cup (175 ml) water

1 cup (200 g) granulated sugar

1 large grapefruit, peeled and pith removed

2 tablespoons (3.4 g) fresh tarragon leaves, roughly chopped

2½ cups (570 ml) freshly squeezed grapefruit juice, strained

TIP › Instead of using only grapefruit juice, try blending entire sections of grapefruit. The puréed pulp will add body and texture to the sorbet.

---

pink grapefruit and tarragon sorbet

This is a versatile sorbet, and when made with in-season, ripe, and very juicy grapefruit, it is a wonderful palate cleanser that will upgrade a meal from fine to fabulous. If tarragon is not a favorite herb, it is easily omitted from the recipe. Consider adding 1 to 2 teaspoons (0.7 to 1.4 g) of chopped, fresh rosemary instead.

Place the water and sugar in a medium-size, heavy-bottomed saucepan and place over medium-high heat. Bring the mixture to a boil while stirring occasionally until the sugar fully dissolves, and continue to boil for about 1 minute. Remove from the heat and set aside to cool, at least 1 hour.

Section the grapefruit into a blender and squeeze the remaining membrane and pith into the blender to extract any remaining juice. Do not add the pith/peel to the blender.

Blend/purée by starting on low speed for a few seconds, then turn to medium speed and blend for about 20 seconds or until smooth. The mixture can retain a small amount of texture as long as it is not overly chunky.

Add the tarragon and blend for another 15 seconds or so—the leaves should be chopped to tiny bits, and they will be visible in the mix.

Add the fresh grapefruit juice and puréed fruit into the cooled syrup and stir well to combine.

Pour into a clean container, cover with a lid or plastic wrap, and chill in the refrigerator for at least 8 hours or overnight.

When ready, pour the chilled mixture into the ice-cream maker and process according to manufacturer's specifications.

Remove the finished sorbet from the ice-cream maker and place in a plastic container. Cover with plastic wrap by pressing the wrap gently against the top of the sorbet, affix lid to container, and place in the freezer to fully harden before serving.

Yield: approximately 1 quart (600 g)

Zest of 3 Meyer lemons

1⅓ cups (267 g) granulated sugar

2¾ cups (650 ml) water

1 cup (240 ml) freshly squeezed Meyer lemon juice, strained (from at least 6 to 7 or more lemons)

meyer lemon sorbet

This sorbet will always remind you of a summer day. Cold and tart, it's the perfect icy treat, both satisfyingly sweet and refreshing like lemonade. For a more intense, fresh lemon flavor, hold aside 1 teaspoon of the lemon zest and add it to the sorbet just before it has finished its freezing cycle. For an "adult" taste of lemonade, add a scoop of the sorbet to a fruity cocktail or glass of champagne!

Place the lemon zest and the sugar in the bowl of a food processor and pulse until it yields fine bits of lemon zest. The mixture may be slightly clumpy due to the moisture from the lemon zest. Transfer to a clean bowl, cover with plastic wrap or a lid, and set aside for 2 hours or overnight.

Place the water and lemon sugar in a medium-size, heavy-bottomed saucepan over medium heat. Bring the mixture to a boil while stirring occasionally until the sugar fully dissolves, and continue to boil for about 1 minute.

Remove from the heat and set aside to cool, at least 1 hour. Stir in the lemon juice, pour into a clean container, cover with a lid or plastic wrap, and chill in the refrigerator for at least 8 hours or overnight.

When ready, pour the chilled mixture into the ice-cream maker and process according to manufacturer's specifications.

Remove the finished sorbet from the ice-cream maker and place in a plastic container. Cover with plastic wrap by pressing the wrap gently against the top of the sorbet, affix lid to container, and place in the freezer to fully harden before serving.

Yield: approximately 1½ quarts (900 g)

{EASY}

2½ cups (570 ml) water

1 cup (200 g) granulated sugar

⅔ cup (60 g) unsweetened, Dutch-processed cocoa powder

7 ounces (200 g) dark chocolate, finely chopped

¼ teaspoon (1.25 ml) pure vanilla extract

Pinch of salt

chocolate sorbet

While not as creamy as its gelato counterpart, chocolate sorbet will satisfy any chocolate lover. Use a dark chocolate with a cocoa percentage of 65 percent or higher to achieve ultimate chocolate intensity, or opt for a lower-percentage milk chocolate if a lighter flavor is desired. For a mocha variation, substitute 2 tablespoons (28 ml) of the water with an equal amount of strongly brewed espresso or add 1 teaspoon espresso powder.

Place the water and sugar in a medium-size, heavy-bottomed saucepan over medium heat. Bring the mixture to a boil while stirring occasionally until the sugar fully dissolves, and continue to boil for about 1 minute.

Whisk in the cocoa powder until fully incorporated. Cook between 180°F and 190°F (82°C and 88°C) for 5 minutes, stirring constantly. Remove from the heat and stir in the chocolate, vanilla, and salt. Stir until smooth and fully combined. Set aside until cool.

Pour into a clean container, cover with a lid or plastic wrap, and chill in the refrigerator for at least 8 hours or overnight.

When ready, pour the chilled mixture into the ice-cream maker and process according to manufacturer's specifications.

Remove the finished sorbet from the ice-cream maker and place in a plastic container. Cover with plastic wrap by pressing the wrap gently against the top of the sorbet, affix lid to container, and place in the freezer to fully harden before serving.

Yield: approximately 1½ quarts (900 g)

{EASY}

4 cups (945 ml) water

1 scant cup (200 g) granulated sugar

3 cups (405 g) roasted hazelnuts, skinned and roughly chopped

Pinch of salt

hazelnut sorbet

In my store, we frequently get requests for hazelnut and other non-fruit-based sorbet. This recipe, while not quite as potent as its gelato counterpart (see page 127), offers nutty goodness in a dairy-free dessert. If roasted hazelnuts are hard to find, buy them raw and toast them in the oven (as directed on page 71).

Place the water and sugar in a medium-size, heavy-bottomed saucepan over medium heat. Bring the mixture to a boil while stirring occasionally until the sugar fully dissolves, and continue to boil for about 1 minute.

Add the hazelnuts and salt, simmer, covered, for 30 minutes. Remove from the heat and set aside to cool for 1 hour.

Process the mixture in a blender or food processor until as smooth as possible. Pour the mixture through a double layer of cheesecloth and into a clean container, wringing as much of the liquid as possible out of the cheesecloth.

Cover with a lid or plastic wrap, and chill in the refrigerator for at least 8 hours or overnight.

When ready, pour the chilled mixture into the ice-cream maker and process according to manufacturer's specifications.

Remove the finished sorbet from the ice-cream maker and place in a plastic container. Cover with plastic wrap by pressing the wrap gently against the top of the sorbet, affix lid to container, and place in the freezer to fully harden before serving.

Yield: approximately 1½ quarts (900 g)

4 cups (945 ml) water

½ cup (100 g) granulated sugar

1½ cups freshly squeezed (355 ml) lime juice

3 tablespoons (45 ml) dark rum

½ cup (12 g) lightly packed

fresh mint leaves

lime-mint granita

This granita is, in essence, a slushy version of the mojito, a popular cocktail. Enjoy it on its own or use it as a palate cleanser between courses for a touch of sophistication at a dinner party.

Pour the water and sugar into a medium-size, heavy-bottomed sauce-pan and place over medium-high heat. Heat, stirring occasionally, until an instant read thermometer registers 160°F (71°C). The mixture should be steaming but not boiling.

Remove from the heat, and set aside until cool, about 1 hour.

When cooled, stir in the lime juice and rum, transfer to a clean 9 x 12-inch (22.5 × 30 cm) shallow baking dish.

Transfer the dish, uncovered, to the freezer. Every 30 minutes, scrape the entire top of the granita from edge to edge with a fork, blending in any ice crystals that have formed. Continue doing this until the granita is completely frozen.

Yield: approximately 1 quart (600 g)

3 cups (710 ml) freshly squeezed orange juice, strained

¼ cup (50 g) granulated sugar

½ cup (120 ml) vodka

screwdriver granita

When the mood calls for a summer cocktail that is more than simply "on the rocks," try this granita. The fresher the orange juice, the more intense the flavor. As a tart, refreshing variation, grapefruit juice can be substituted.

Pour the orange juice and sugar into a medium-size, heavy-bottomed saucepan and place over medium-high heat. Heat, stirring occasionally, until an instant-read thermometer registers 160°F (71°C). The mixture should be steaming but not boiling.

Remove from the heat, and set aside until cool, about 1 hour.

When cooled, stir in the vodka, transfer to clean 9 × 12-inch (22.5 × 30 cm) shallow baking dish, cover, and refrigerate for 6 hours or overnight.

Transfer the dish, uncovered, to the freezer. Every 30 minutes, scrape the entire top of the granita from edge to edge with a fork, blending in any ice crystals that have formed. Continue doing this until the granita is completely frozen.

Yield: approximately 1 quart (600 g)

blue cheese granita with poached pears

This recipe elegantly turns a savory food into a dessert. The nontraditional granita served with poached pears merges two traditional flavors in one unique presentation. When making a savory granita such as this one, be sure to use a main ingredient with an intense natural flavor that will not be diluted by the addition of so much water.

{EASY}

FOR THE GRANITA:

3 cups (710 ml) water

2 tablespoons (40 g) honey

2 tablespoons (28 ml) vodka

1 cup (120 g) crumbled blue cheese

¼ cup (30 g) raw walnuts, chopped medium fine

FOR THE POACHED PEARS:

3 cups (710 ml) water

3 cups (710 ml) red or white wine

¾ cup (150 g) sugar

¼ cup (60 ml) freshly squeezed lemon juice, strained

1½ teaspoons (2.5 g) black peppercorns, cracked

1 cinnamon stick

4 firm, ripe pears (Bosc or Anjou), peeled and cored

To make the granita: Pour the water and honey into a medium-size, heavy-bottomed saucepan and place over medium-high heat. Heat, stirring occasionally, until an instant-read thermometer registers 160°F (71°C). The mixture should be steaming but not boiling. Remove from the heat, and set aside until cool, about 1 hour.

When cooled, stir in the vodka, transfer to clean container, cover, and refrigerate 6 hours or overnight.

Remove the mixture from the refrigerator and pour into the container of a heavy-duty blender or a food processor fitted with the blade attachment.

While processing on medium speed, add 1 cup of blue cheese in four increments, blending until well combined.

Pour the blended mixture into a clean mixing bowl and fold in the walnuts. Pour into a clean 9 x 12-inch (22.5 x 32.5 cm) shallow baking dish and transfer, uncovered, to the freezer. Every 30 minutes, take a fork and scrape the entire top of the granita from edge to edge, blending in any ice crystals that have formed. Continue doing this until the granita is completely frozen.

Yield: approximately 3 cups (450 g)

To make the poached pears: Combine first 6 ingredients in a large saucepan and place over low heat. Add the pears and poach at a gentle simmer for approximately ½ hour, until the pears are tender to the touch but not mushy. This may take slightly more or less time depending on the ripeness of the pears used.

Remove from the heat and cool in the poaching liquid, about 4 hours. Pour into a clean container, cover, transfer to the refrigerator. Chill overnight, covered, until ready to use or up to 3 days.

To serve: Remove the pears from liquid and slice in half. Core using a melon baller or paring knife. Place on a plate and top with blue cheese granita.

strawberry sorbet with balsamic drizzle

Strawberries and balsamic vinegar combine naturally, as the sweetness of the strawberries offsets the slight sting of the vinegar. Because the flavor of the vinegar is paramount, always use one of very good quality, which can be somewhat costly. However, the expense is well worth the outcome and the vinegar can be used in many other recipes. The recipe for balsamic drizzle included here is a substitute for very good-quality balsamic vinegar, in case that is not available.

{MEDIUM}

FOR THE SORBET:

2¾ pounds (1.25 kg)
fresh strawberries, cleaned
and hulled

¾ cup (150 g) granulated sugar

2 teaspoons (10 ml) freshly
squeezed and strained lemon
juice

1 cup (240 ml) water

2 tablespoons (40 g) all-natural
strawberry preserves or jam

FOR THE BALSAMIC DRIZZLE:

2 cups (475 ml) balsamic
vinegar

1 dried fig, stem removed

2 juniper berries

1 black peppercorn

2 tablespoons (40 g) honey

To make the strawberry sorbet: Place the strawberries and sugar in a bowl and toss to combine. Cover with plastic wrap or a lid and place in the refrigerator overnight, stirring occasionally to incorporate the sugar and strawberry juices.

Place the macerated strawberries into a blender or the bowl of a food processor, add the lemon juice, and purée until smooth. Set aside until ready to use.

Place the water and preserves in a medium-size, heavy-bottomed saucepan and place over medium heat. Bring the mixture to a boil while stirring occasionally until the preserves fully dissolve, and continue to boil for about 1 minute. Remove from the heat and set aside to cool, at least 1 hour.

Add the strawberry purée into the cooled syrup and stir well to combine. Pour into a clean container, cover with a lid or plastic wrap, and chill in the refrigerator for at least 8 hours or overnight.

When ready, pour the chilled mixture into the ice-cream maker and process according to manufacturer's specifications.

Remove the finished sorbet from the ice-cream maker and place in a plastic container. Cover with plastic wrap by pressing the wrap gently against the top of the sorbet, affix lid to container, and place in the freezer to fully harden before serving.

Yield: approximately 1½ quarts (900 g)

To make the balsamic drizzle: Combine all ingredients in a small, heavy-bottomed saucepan over medium heat and bring to a boil. Reduce the heat and simmer until the mixture is reduced by half and is the consistency of maple syrup. Remove from the heat and set aside to cool. The drizzle can be stored in an airtight container in the refrigerator for up to two months.

toppings and sauces

What would gelato and sorbet be (or any frozen dessert, for that matter) without delicious toppings and mix-ins? These recipes liberate you from the standard, store-bought, preservative-laden toppings that you are familiar with. Most of the classics are here, but add whatever you like best! One of the parting messages of this book is to be bold, and there is no such thing as a "wrong" topping, just as long as you like it!

⅔ cup (160 ml) heavy cream

½ cup (176 g) light corn syrup

¼ cup (23 g) unsweetened Dutch-processed cocoa powder

⅓ cup (75 g) packed light brown sugar

4 ounces (115 g) milk chocolate

2 ounces (55 g) bittersweet chocolate

2 tablespoons (28 g) salted butter

½ teaspoon (2.5 ml) pure vanilla extract

fudge sauce

This fudge sauce is easy to make and is sure to become an all-around favorite. Although it has a strong chocolate flavor, this sauce is not as intense as many others. To boost its chocolate essence, use all dark chocolate instead of a mixture of milk and dark.

Place the cream, corn syrup, cocoa powder, brown sugar, and milk chocolate in a medium-size, heavy-bottomed saucepan over medium heat. Stir to combine and bring the mixture to a boil. Lower the heat and simmer for approximately 5 minutes, stirring occasionally.

Remove from the heat and add the dark chocolate, butter, and vanilla extract. Stir until fully dissolved and combined.

Allow the sauce to cool slightly before serving.

The sauce will keep in an airtight container in the refrigerator for up to 2 weeks. Warm before serving.

Yield: approximately 2 cups (608 g)

½ cup (120 ml) heavy cream

¾ cup (175 ml) whole milk

½ pound (225 g) dark chocolate, finely chopped

1 tablespoon (14 g) unsalted butter

chocolate sauce

This sauce offers a dose of chocolate flavor but in a lighter texture than the Fudge Sauce. If the sauce seems too thick after it has cooled, additional milk or heavy cream can be whisked in, 1 tablespoon (15 ml) at a time, until the desired consistency is reached.

Place the cream and milk in a small, heavy-bottomed saucepan placed over medium heat and bring to a boil.

Remove from the heat and stir in the chocolate until smooth and homogenous.

Whisk in the butter until fully combined.

Allow the sauce to cool slightly before serving.

The sauce will keep for up to 2 weeks in an airtight container in the refrigerator. Warm before serving if desired.

Yield: approximately 1½ cups (450 g)

2 cups (475 ml) heavy cream

½ cup (120 ml) water

1 cup (200 g) granulated sugar

Pinch of salt

1 teaspoon (5 ml) pure vanilla extract

caramel sauce

Working with hot caramel syrup can be challenging. If you have never made caramel before, pay attention and proceed slowly and carefully. (See Caramel Gelato, page 132, for tips on working with caramel.) For a variation, substitute 3 tablespoons (45 ml) of bourbon for the vanilla. Also, for a buttery- flavored sauce, stir in 2 tablespoons (28 g) of butter with the vanilla or bourbon.

Place the cream in a small, heavy-bottomed saucepan over medium heat and bring to a simmer. Remove from the heat and set aside until ready to use.

Place the water and sugar in a deep, heavy-bottomed saucepan over medium-high heat and bring to a boil, stirring occasionally. Insert a candy thermometer and cook the mixture until a candy thermometer registers 345°F (174°C) degrees. The mixture will begin to turn a reddish brown, mahogany color.

Remove from the heat, remove the candy thermometer, and, very carefully and slowly, add half of the warm cream to the hot caramel mixture. As the cream is being added, the caramel will bubble up, almost to a rolling boil. When this has subsided, add the remaining warm cream and whisk until thoroughly combined.

Stir in the salt and vanilla extract. Allow the sauce to cool slightly before serving.

The sauce will keep for up to 2 weeks in an airtight container in the refrigerator. If the sauce thickens up in the refrigerator, it can be reheated slightly to thin before serving.

Yield: approximately 2¼ cups (738 g)

{EASY}

chocolate chip cookie mix-in

4 tablespoons (55 g) butter

¼ cup (55 g) coconut oil

¼ cup (60 g) dark brown sugar

½ cup (176 g) light corn syrup

1 teaspoon (5 ml) pure vanilla extract

1¼ cups (156 g) all-purpose flour

⅛ teaspoon (0.8 g) salt

1 cup (170 g) mini chocolate chips

True cookie dough fiends understand the attraction to adding cookie dough to just about everything. This dough can be stirred into gelato while placing the gelato into a dish to harden in the freezer, as most home ice–cream makers aren't powerful enough to blend in the cookie dough when the gelato has frozen and thickened up.

Combine the butter, coconut oil, and dark brown sugar in a mixing bowl and cream together in a stand mixer or with a hand mixer until smooth and fluffy.

Add the corn syrup and vanilla extract, and mix to combine. In a separate bowl, stir together the flour and salt.With your mixer on low speed, gently add the flour to the butter mixture, and mix until just combined. Fold in the chocolate chips.

Transfer dough to a piece of waxed paper, cover with plastic wrap, and place in the refrigerator for 30 minutes.

Remove from the refrigerator and roll out the dough into a rope approximately ½ inch (1.25 cm) in diameter. Using a sharp knife, cut into pieces ½ inch (1.25 cm) long, transfer to a chilled baking sheet, and put into your freezer to harden until ready for use.

{EASY}

12 ounces (340 g) fine-quality semisweet chocolate

8 tablespoons (112 g, or 1 stick) unsalted butter, at room temperature

¼ cup (60 ml) canola oil

⅓ cup plus 1 tablespoon (280 g) granulated sugar

6 eggs

1 cup (110 g) cake flour

Confectioners' sugar

brownie mix-ins

These brownies are customized to be ideal for mixing into gelato or ice cream of any flavor. They have more oil than a normal brownie, which keeps them softer and chewier when they're frozen. A standard brownie in gelato, while still delicious, tends to become soggy and lose some of its trademark fudge-like quality.

Preheat oven to 350°F (177°C). Line a 9 × 13-inch (22.5 × 32.5 cm) baking pan with parchment or waxed paper. Butter and flour the parchment and sides of the pan.

Chop or break chocolate into small pieces. Melt in a microwave or in a heavy-bottomed saucepan over low heat. Stir until smooth. Pour into mixer bowl. Cool slightly, until just warm to the touch.

Beat butter and oil into warm chocolate. Beat in sugar. Add eggs one at a time, beating until mixture lightens. Blend in flour on low speed. Do not overmix.

Pour into pan. Bake at 350°F (180°C, or gas mark 4) for 35 to 40 minutes or until center is almost set. Cool in pan. Run a knife around edges and remove whole, baked brownie from the pan. Transfer to a baking sheet, place in the freezer, and freeze until hard. Remove from the freezer, remove parchment paper, and cut into small dice. Freeze diced pieces until they are ready to incorporate into gelato.

Yield: Makes about 20 brownies, before dicing

2½ tablespoons (20 g) arrowroot or Clear-Jel

¼ cup (50 g) sugar

2 cups (290 g) fruit, frozen or fresh

1 cup (240 ml) water

1 teaspoon (5 ml) freshly squeezed lemon juice, strained

TIP › I prefer to use Clear-Jel or arrowroot to cornstarch. Both Clear-Jel and arrowroot are more refined starches and, consequently, result in a thick sauce without the starchy taste that cornstarch may leave if it is not properly cooked.

berry topping

This fruit topping is reminiscent of fruit pie filling in its consistency. Not as sweet, however, it makes a delightful topping for gelato. Blueberries, raspberries, blackberries, strawberries, or a combination thereof all work well.

The cooking process breaks down the fruit into a smooth sauce. A chunkier consistency is attained by cooking only 1 cup (145 g) of the fruit, then adding the remaining fruit during the final 5 minutes of cooking.

Combine the arrowroot starch and sugar in a mixing bowl and whisk together to incorporate and disperse the arrowroot starch evenly in the sugar.

Place fruit in a medium-size, heavy-bottomed saucepan, add the sugar mixture, and stir to coat; cover fruit.

Add the water and place saucepan over medium heat.

Stirring constantly, slowly bring the mixture up to a "boil" (due to its thick nature, the mixture won't actually boil but will give the illusion of doing so).

Once the fruit is bubbling, lower the heat slightly and cook for an additional 4 minutes. The sauce should become clear.

Once the fruit sauce is no longer opaque, taste it to make sure that it does not have a lingering starchy taste. If it does, continue cooking for a couple of minutes longer. Remove the sauce from the heat once it is clear and no starchy taste remains, and allow to cool to room temperature.

Incorporate the lemon juice, pour into a clean container, and allow to fully cool in the refrigerator.

The sauce will keep for up to 1 week in an airtight container in the refrigerator. You can use it cold or you can warm before serving.

Yield: approximately 2½ cups (850 g)

Nut Brittle

2 cups (400 g) sugar

½ cup (120 ml) water

1 stick (110 g) unsalted butter

1/3 cup (120 g) corn syrup

¼ teaspoon baking soda

1/2 teaspoon kosher salt

14 ounces (397 g) lightly-toasted pecans

A sweet-and-savory treat on its own, nut brittle is a delectable topping for any of the recipes in this book. Replace the pecans with any number of toasted nuts for other elegant serving ideas.

Combine the sugar, water, butter, and corn syrup in a large sauce pan and bring to a boil. Cook over medium high heat, stirring occasionally, until the mixture registers 300°F (149°C) on a candy thermometer. Remove from heat and stir in the baking soda and salt. The mixture will bubble. Stir in the nuts and quickly scrape the mixture on to a rimmed baking sheet lined with a silpat silicone nonstick mat, or parchment paper, sprayed lightly with nonstick cooking spray. Working quickly, spread the mixture into an even layer. Let cool completely before breaking it into pieces.

resources

Sources and Recommended Reading

Gelato. Pamela Sheldon Johns and Jennifer Barry Design. Copyright 2000. Ten Speed Press.

The Ultimate Frozen Dessert Book. Weinstein, Bruce & Scarbrough, Mark. Copyright 2005. William Morrow, Harper Collins.

The Ultimate Ice Cream Book. Weinsten, Bruce. Copyright 1999. William Morrow, Harper Collins.

The Perfect Scoop. Lebovitz, David. Copyright 2007. Ten Speed Press.

Ice Cream. 6th edition. Marshall, Robert; Goff, Doug; Hartel, Richard. Copyright 2003. Plenum Publishers.

On Food & Cooking. McGee, Harold. 2nd Edition. Copyright 2004. Scribner.

Los Secretos del Helado. Corvitto, Angelo. Copyright 2004. Grupo Vilbo Publishers.

The Science of Ice Cream. Clarke, Chris. Copyright 2004. RSC Publishing.

Freddo e Gelato. Giacobbi, Roberto. Gruppo Etabeta Editoriale.

Ice Cream and Frozen Desserts. Stogo, Malcolm. Copyright 1998. John Wiley & Sons.

Cookwise. Corriher, Shirley. Copyright 1997. William Morrow Harper Collins.

Essentials of Classic Italian Cooking. Hazan, Marcella. Copyright 1992. Alfred Knopf, Inc.

How to Read a French Fry. Parsons, Russ. Copyright 2001. Houghton Mifflin.

Williams Sonoma
Williamssonoma.com
General kitchen equipment and supplies

Sur la Table
Surlatable.com
General kitchen equipment and supplies

Knife Merchant
Knifemerchant.com
Great selection of every knife you've ever imagined

Chocosphere
www.chocosphere.com
Chocolate from all over the world

Newport Specialty Foods
newportspecialtyfoods.com
A wide assortment of specialty ingredients

Kitchen Aid
www.kitchenaid.com
Ice cream makers, blenders (immersion and regular)

Cuisinart
www.cuisinart.com
Ice cream makers, food processors and immersion blenders

World Spice Merchants
www.worldspice.com
Freshest Spices

www.saltworks.us
Varied selection of sea salts for creating salty and sweet combinations

www.eguittard.com
High-quality chocolate and cocoa powder

www.rivalproducts.com
Manufacturer of the old-fashioned ice and salt ice-cream maker

www.frontiercoop.com
Organic extracts and flavors, essential oils

Chef's Choice
www.edgecraft.com
Ice-cream cone maker

index

acknowledgments

I would like to thank a number of people who made this book possible. First, thanks to Tina for all of her help in getting me through the writing process and for keeping me (somewhat) focused on the tasks at hand, as well as for interpreting my somewhat-less-than-clear recipe intentions.

Thanks also to Madeline for her infinite patience with my complete lack of organization when it came to the photo shoots, and for still managing to make the gelato look so beautiful. Thanks to my mother, Marcia, for her exhaustive recipe testing and extraordinarily detailed feedback.

A special thank you goes to all my incredible employees at Cold Fusion Gelato, for staying on top of everything while I embarked on this project. On a professional front, thanks to Kathy and the gang at Newport Specialty Foods for keeping me supplied with a never-ending source of ingredients during the recipe development process; thanks to John McCabe and the folks at Carpigiani USA for all of their equipment assistance and expertise, and finally, thanks to John Yodice at Fabbri North America for being a constant source of help and advice from that first day six years ago when I thought about gelato for the very first time. I would also be remiss if I failed to thank my editor Rochelle Bourgault, who must be the most patient person on earth for putting up with my continued organizational ineptitude and utter failure to meet deadlines on anything even remotely resembling a timely basis.

And last but definitely not least, I'd like to thank Nola, for her love, support, and unwavering belief in both me and in this oft-seeming quixotic gelato dream of ours.